The Trip of My Life

By
Mary Lamb Lucas

Dedication

This book is dedicated to my son Trip, whose baptized name was Joseph Henry Lucas III.

I knew him and loved him before he was born. He was loving, handsome, smart, physically gifted and a kind, encouraging son. When he was about eighteen months old and sitting on a small wooden giraffe with wheels, wearing a blue bib topped by a straw sombrero on his head, I said to myself, "he is so cute, we just have to do this again." That meant to have another child. It was a nice surprise that he was followed by four younger sisters, two sets of twin girls in the next three and a half years.

Acknowledgment

As it is often said, "It takes a village to raise a child." In my case, that was true for Trip. I am grateful for those who were the village who helped raise Trip. One of those is Townley Chisholm, who was Trip's ninth grade science teacher, and the leader of St. Christopher School's outdoor program. Because of that he was responsible for introducing Trip to rock climbing. Climbing became an activity that was Trip's favorite. Townley became a mentor and good friend to Trip from St. Christopher's onward. Townley led the celebration of Trip's life that took place at The University of Virginia Chapel. Susan and Peter Bance loved Trip, employed him at their farm, and encouraged him in countless ways. Peter is the one who was able to keep Trip from taking his life when his marriage ended. Chris Van Dusen Butler and her husband, Ellis, were Trip's good friends from days at UVA until Trip's last day.

The village that helped to raise this book began with a clue from Constance Costas whom I met the New Year's Eve that I had just begun. She suggested I go to a workshop with well-known author and teacher, Dani Shapiro. Dani led my first writing conference, which was my intro to being in a group with other writers. She suggested I apply to Aspen Words' juried workshops and taught the first one I attended. Pilar Garcia Brown is an editor who gave me an excellent line edit at that first workshop. Adrienne Brodeur, the executive director of Aspen Words, has been an amazing inspiration through Aspen Words and as a writer.

Hedgebrook introduced me to writing teacher, Theo Nestor, who read my manuscript and made invaluable suggestions and comments.

I cannot overlook the Glenwood Writers in Glenwood Springs, Colorado. They and the fellow writers at Aspen Words workshops opened my mind to the realization that horses are not the only ones who are some of my favorite people. I found that writers are also some of my favorite people. Having lunch on the outside deck of an Aspen Words' workshop one day, just watching and listening to writers, it dawned on me that I liked these people.

Nor can I overlook my local bookstore, the Bookworm of Edwards, Colorado. It is the best. It was begun by Nicole Magistro, another book-raiser – she of the willing ear and world of book wisdom that she has shared with me. My sister Antoinette (Auntoinette to the kids), and my late sister Betsy have both been generously keeping me in Bookworm gift cards. There's Holly Proctor the publisher of my neighborhood magazine and General Encourager when it comes to the magazine and/or stirring up neighborhood fun. Will Theorharides, artist extraordinaire, who's made an adoring fan of me with his kind ways and helpfulness. Then there are the friends and neighbors who, like Dale and Jeannie Mosier, have never failed to ask "how's the book coming?" almost every time we meet. How could it have been born without all of them? I am forever grateful for all these walking talking "bookangels".

About the Author

MaryLamb Lucas was born and raised in West Virginia. She migrated to Virginia for college where she met the man she married and had five children, a son and two sets of twin daughters. She is an experienced parent and psychotherapist who has always loved to write. As a child, she was inspired by Little House on the Prairie when her teacher read it to the whole third grade class. MaryLamb began her own version of it at age 8. Her Mother quashed that when she objected to an adjective describing the mother in the book. Within the next year or two, MaryLamb published and distributed a neighborhood newspaper and wrote poetry all before she finished sixth grade.

While raising her five children, MaryLamb volunteered for the Junior League of Richmond, Virginia, and contributed articles to the Junior League newsletter. She also wrote a column for the local newspaper in the rural county where she lived.

Her post child-raising years involved writing classes at Virginia Commonwealth University and The Virginia Museum of Fine Arts along with writing conferences and workshops. She also went to graduate school to become a Jungian oriented psychotherapist. When the kids left home after college, her marriage ended, and she moved her life and therapy practice to Colorado.

Her son, Trip, inspired her memoir when he took his own life at age 48. She has workshopped the memoir at Aspen Words workshops, some other writing courses, and retreats, and with a local writing group.

In addition to always wanting to be a writer and a mom, horses were some of MaryLamb's favorite people and were a part of her life for a very long time. No horses followed her when she moved to

Colorado and traded her riding boots for ski boots but she still considers them some of her favorite people.

Table of Contents

"I had two sets of younger twin sisters by the time I was three. I believe I had some abandonment issues from losing my mom's full-time attention at two and then again at three. I resented that they followed me around like ducklings watching everything I did for a time. I even quit riding for a while because I didn't like them all sitting on the fence watching me get lessons in our pastures. They always destroyed my comic books. Did I mention that I have to keep working on forgiveness? I wish I could have a do-over. I could have been a much better brother. It was fun to be able to go drinking and climbing and skiing with them after college."

25 Random Things About Me. #23 Trip Lucas, Facebook.

Chapter One

It was dark on a September night in 2014 when my oldest of five children and only son, 48-year-old Trip, called me. I loved hearing his voice, with what was usually a warm, friendly "Hi, Mom." It's deep and a mix of sensitivity, energy, and smarts with a whiff of humor.

"Hi, sweetie," I said.

"What're you doing?" He asked in a quiet voice. I could tell he was not driving like he often was when he called. He must be at his home in Austin, Texas.

"Just driving home from a meeting with a friend in the car," I said to him so he would realize that he was probably on speaker. The sky was a clear, cloudless dark, which revealed stars bright as diamonds over the Eagle River valley.

"What's up?" I said.

"Oh nothing," same quiet voice.

"Shall I call you back when I get home?"

"No, I can't even remember why I called."

Something in his voice worried me and told me to call him back anyway. His not wanting to talk with my friend in the car said to me that he had something important and personal to discuss. But I forgot to call him when I got in. I was exhausted, and sleep took over.

I had been ambivalent about the big volunteer effort that the evening's meeting had been about. It ran well past dark, which was late for me. I get up early and go to bed early. There's pressure on locals to volunteer to help "showcase our community to a global audience through arts, athletics, and education." The pressure to conform, too reminiscent of my traumatic and unloving childhood, was what bothered me.

I was in the eighth year of the second chapter of starting my life over. The first chapter was the 12 years between the end of my marriage when I established myself as a self-employed psychotherapist and then left Virginia for Colorado. At this point, I was in Colorado. Most of the time, I felt liberated, even exhilarated, but there were a few moments when I was not quite wanting to rise to the occasion. This volunteer effort was one of them. I was still a fulltime psychotherapist and only had so much free time. And there was my resistance to the pressure from authority.

In the morning, I was getting ready for a dental appointment when the phone rang. It was Trip.

"Mom," he said, "Laura is breaking up with me, and I don't think I can live through another break-up."

White noise filled my head. No! I thought, but then I told myself that he was older now. At 48, he couldn't be as devastated and near self-destruction as he was when his marriage to Kim dissolved. Now he knew that life goes on. Laura was the woman he had been living with for the past five years.

"Oh, honey, yes, you can," I said. "There are too many people who love you. You can't leave them."

"Mom, this isn't about you."

My stomach dropped a couple of feet. I didn't know what to say.

"Trip…"

"I went to a doctor and got a prescription for an anti-depressant," he continued. "I took one this morning."

"That's great; I'm glad you did," the therapist in me answered. "You know it might take a couple of weeks to take effect?"

"Uh huh," he said, "I'm on Lexapro."

"That's a good one."

He told me he just wanted to go to Laura's work and...

"What?" I asked. I thought he wanted to show her how much he was hurting over this impending break-up by hurting or killing himself, which scared me down to my bones. He didn't say. He complained that the phone connection was sketchy. It *was* sketchy. AT&T was having problems and not doing much to solve them. So many of us depended on our cell phones entirely, having given up our landlines. It's the cell towers that were not doing their job. I was walking in and out of my closet, pulling out clothes and putting them on as we talked. Suddenly, I realized my legs were weak. I was becoming paralyzed by fear. My family legacy of fear, shame/bad-me feelings erupted from within. They caused me to lose faith in my own voice, my own knowing, dissociate, leave, be afraid, deny what needed to be done right then - any or all - of those things. At that moment, it's how I was – all of it.

My head was spinning and, in a year or more from now, I would admit to myself that not standing up to the moment was how I had dealt with life, especially the scary parts. As a psychotherapist in private practice, I had never been interested in being on the other end of a hotline, the emergency thing. Some people loved it. I was not interested. It scared me because of my family of origin that was not loving, always on edge, frightening with the drinking and loud, often physically violent, arguments between my parents. The belittling and shaming things they said to me were included. I would be rattled and not thinking clearly. I would just want the violence and anger to stop.

Even though I *knew* the first thing to ask a person thinking of suicide is if he has a plan, I convinced myself that if Trip had gotten an anti-depressant, he wasn't at the edge yet, and I could get back to him after the dentist. Maybe then the cell service would be better. Scared me. Petrified me.

"Sweetie, I'd better go if I'm going to make the dentist appointment. Can I call you back later?"

There I went, running away from my fear, from the moment and worst of all, *from Trip.*

"Uh huh."

"I love you."

"Mmph."

I sank into a chair in the dentist's waiting room, feeling afraid. I was worried about Trip and how hard a break-up was for him. My smart, fun, funny, handsome son who had so many gifts from the universe but just couldn't handle abandonment and a breakup. No, no, no, I couldn't think about that. This couldn't happen. It just couldn't.

If he hadn't come home to live with me after his marriage broke up –several years before, I was pretty sure he wouldn't have made it then. He had confessed to a family friend, Peter, who loved Trip, how he was feeling and that he wanted to shoot himself. Peter talked Trip into coming home from Austin to stay with me back in Virginia. My little house was near where the kids grew up. I was just beginning my recovery after divorce and years of a lonely and not-so-good marriage. When Trip arrived, it was a good time for both of us. He stayed for nine months, got part time jobs he liked, recovered his balance, and went on to re-discover his life.

I told my hygienist, who had become a friend that I was worried about my son but didn't tell her how dire it could be. When her hands weren't in my mouth, I stared out the window at the familiar alpine landscape, white noise back in my head. My whole body was in a knot.

Afterward, as I headed toward my car, I saw a message from Laura, who was in Austin, and a voicemail from my daughter Kate in Virginia. Damn, AT&T – my phone didn't make a peep in the dentist's office. I sat in the car, checking my messages. I saw Laura's text,

"Call your son NOW." My stomach dropped again.

I listened to Kate's voicemail. She said that Trip was threatening to shoot himself and that she had gotten him to talk, but he hung up on her when Laura called, and he switched over to talk with Laura. I started to go numb again. My chest was tight, and my breath came in hard, short gasps. Kate hadn't been able to reach Trip or Laura since. Kate is one of my older set of twins, the fraternal ones. She's the brown-eyed one.

I tried to call Kate back, and to call Trip, but no cell phone service again. Dammit. Panicking, I drove a few miles east until I got service, but then I remembered my five-month-old puppy, Bijou. I didn't want to leave her in her crate any longer. I made the ten-minute round trip to go home and get her. Bijou and I drove a few minutes to the next town over, Avon, where I had cell service. I parked to the side of Starbucks and made another attempt at calls. I waited, hoping to hear something. Something good. Again, I tried both Trip and Laura without success.

Finally, I tried Kate again – no luck - and then Dana, my daughter in Idaho. She is one of the younger, identical set of twins. Dana has heard what was happening but had not talked with me until now or with Trip. I had the sinking feeling that we were too late. I wanted to scream "no!" but who was going to hear it? What difference would it make?

Dana wanted to start calling hospitals near Trip, hoping he was at one of them, alive and not seriously injured. I hoped she was right that he could be stopped before he did anything permanent. But his father - Joe - taught all the kids how to handle guns, to shoot skeet, and he took Trip duck hunting. After college, Trip did a stint in the Army. He was not likely to make a mistake.

The wait was excruciating. I read somewhere long ago that a woman's traditional lot had been to wait. To wait for the baby to be born, for the husband and kids to come home, for the outcomes of games or spelling bees, for the news of how your kid was after he got hurt. I became more afraid that Trip was going to kill himself or that he had already.

I thought about Trip and who he was. At 48, he was a kind and loving son and man, proficient in French, Italian, and Chinese. He had spent time in both France and Italy and other places in Western Europe. He loved it there. He had been in the Army for two years – at this father's urging. It sent him to the Defense Language Institute and taught him Chinese. He was an excellent athlete, proficient in several sports. He loved to travel, meet people, and have friends all over the world. He was a good-looking guy who had yet to meet "the one" and had no children. He had married for a short time, but his wife, Kim, already had the only child she wanted, and then the marriage didn't last. He had some maturing yet to do, and I think he wanted kids. At least he and Laura thought about having one. He liked women, though, and they were attracted to him. I thought he would be a good father.

I will always remember the day when he was 11. We were in the car, heading out of our driveway. It encircled the grass-covered center with its pair of geriatric walnut trees and the young magnolia tree I had planted. I was taking him to cotillion.

He said, "Mom, there's something I want to talk to you about. It's about girls."

 "Have you decided that you like them?" I said.

"No, but I'm starting to notice," he said.

He also liked kids and animals, was smart and athletic, and was a good wrestler and soccer player in high school. He participated in the school's outdoor program with canoeing, rock-climbing, hiking and more. He became a rock-climber who climbed with some of the best. He often went to a place in Mexico, Potrero Chico, which is one of the places where many sponsored climbers go to climb. When he was younger, he rode horses, belonged to Pony Club, and fox hunted (on ponies/horses) like all his sisters and many of the kids who lived near us out in the country.

The next place I really want to climb is Railay beach in Thailand.

25 Random Things About Me #7. Trip Lucas, Facebook

He had his MBA in information management and was proficient at a particular software, but he had been struggling to find a good job in his field. It was a complicated issue. There was a successful tech bigwig who had bought up most of the contracts for information management jobs. He turned them into six-month contracts with no benefits and no continuing education. If a man like Trip, with the degree and the skills took one of those jobs, then he had to look for another one when that job was done, or the six months were up. He would be out of work, with no benefits whatsoever, and would have to look for another job. It was not the road to a life of well-being. It was, literally, a grind, and then you die. In Trip's case, there were at least two different companies who got to know him and his work under a contract situation and liked him and his work enough to want to buy out his contract. Then, they could keep him as a full-time employee. In one case the headhunter that found the job for Trip wanted an exorbitant amount for him, so the company backed down. In the other case, there was something equally difficult that scotched that job Trip might have had. Trip really liked the idea of the first one. He would have been living in Germany, but he was fine with that. He already liked the Germans with whom he was working.

Trip was an engaging person. When he and two of his sisters, Antoinette and Dana, were here in July, the three of them subbed in my weekly old folks' tennis game. It was the Fourth of July weekend, and several of the regulars were away visiting family. The games were always fun and full of laughter. The kids fit right in. Afterward, one of the regulars came up to me and said, "MaryLamb, your kids are good people." That made my heart swell. I already thought so, like most moms do. It was nice to hear it from someone else, though. My kids *are* good people.

There was a skinny Aspen tree next to where I was parked. I took Bijou out of the car to let her pee. She was quiet as if she was reflecting my somber mood. Sitting there, I remembered coming home one afternoon in July when Trip was here. He was outside in the yard with Bijou. As I walked toward them, Trip whispered, "Bijou just watched a bird for at least five minutes." It was a sweet, magical moment, seeing him appreciate her toddling discovery of the world. I was touched when that happened, and later, outside Starbucks, tears puddled. How could my sweet, sensitive, puppy-watching son, with his zest and reverence for life, think he was not worth living?

Trip had been living in Austin, Texas, most of the time since he finished his two years in the Army. He got his International MBA at the University of Texas, which enabled him to get a job with an international corporation that sent him to France. To go abroad is exactly why he got the International MBA. In undergrad at UVA, he majored in French, took Italian as his second language, and spent part of his third year of college at a university in Aix en Provence, France.

Later, when the job in France ended, the company wanted him to find another job within it, but that meant he'd be living in New York. The city life didn't appeal to him, so he returned to Austin.

At my wit's end, I called Topper. He is a hometown friend of mine who lived in Austin. By the time of Trip's desperation, he knew Trip, Laura, and all four of my daughters. He knew Kim, Trip's wife, too. "What can I do to help?" he asked. "Would you please go to Trip and Laura's house to see if you can find out anything?" "Of course," he said.

———

*"Children not loved for who they are never learn to love themselves. Their growth
is an exercise in pleasing others, not expanding through experience. As adults,
they must learn to nurture their own lost child."*
~ Marion Woodman

As I was writing this a few years later, I felt a state of helplessness that took me back not only to that moment of Trip's, but to many childhood moments when my drunken parents were fighting. They would both be enraged, but Daddy was stronger than Mother, and his rage was more frightening to me. I had seen him hurt Mother and give her bruises that lasted for days. I would be terrified and want them to stop, but I had no power to make that happen. There was one time when one of their late, post-party fights was raging in their bedroom. It woke me up. I tiptoed around to the crack in their bedroom door that was a little warped and didn't shut completely. What I saw was a dark-haired, drunk daddy in pajamas chasing a blond, also drunk mother in her nightgown around the bedroom with a pillow in his hand, rage in his eyes and voice. He wanted to hurt her. I was frightened enough that I ran, in the dark, the mile or so to my grandparents' house. I woke them up, banging on their door, saying, "Help, help, he's going to kill her!" I was in grade school then.

On ordinary weekdays when we lived in that house where we were when I was 4 to 12, mornings started with me and mother in the kitchen. Mother would be fixing breakfast, and Daddy would be upstairs getting dressed for work. When he was almost ready, he would stomp on the floor in their bedroom above the kitchen to let mother know he was on his way down. It would make mother so furious that she would take the broom and poke the ceiling back at Daddy, screwing up her mouth, teeth crossed – the way she looked when angry. It may sound like a funny scene, but it wasn't funny at the time. Their anger frightened me and made me shrink into myself. Over time, I became mute, unable to say much of anything, a frightened, empty shell. It's one of the reasons I became a therapist. My sister Antoinette became a therapist, too. The other reason has to do with not being loved by my parents. Not only did they not love us, but they shamed and belittled us. Mother's insults and shaming were more frequent. As for Daddy, he was at his office during the week, but his temper and anger scared the wits out of me when he was home. I believed that I was unlovable and was *bad* and unworthy of being loved. I avoided both parents and shared as little as possible with them. I must have thought that was the best way to not have confrontations. To complicate things, I was a daydreamer and often lost in my daydreams, dawdling at whatever I was supposed to be doing.

I meandered and daydreamed my way to school so that I'd often be late. At age 7, in second grade, I must have started to get embarrassed about walking in late to school. One day, I was late; heaven knows what I had been dreaming about that day, but the day before a friend's dog had run behind me when I left her house, running toward home because it was almost dinner time. As I ran, her dog scratched the back of one of my legs with his toenail. It was a deep scratch. At school the next morning, I told the teacher that a dog had bitten me on the way to school and showed her the scratch. What ensued was a liar's worst nightmare. Rabies had been going around in the dog world. The school called home. After my mother's consultation with the pediatrician, my father left his office to pick me up and drive me around to see if we could find the dog that "bit" me. I heard that the treatment for someone bitten by a rabid dog was 14 shots in the abdomen. What if not finding the dog would result in my being given the shots just in case? I kept my mouth shut anyway. The dog wasn't found, and I did not have to get the shots.

———

Hours had passed – maybe three, four. I was still outside Starbucks. Over and over, cars pulled in and left. Finally, there was a call. It was Topper, at Trip's, to tell me that Trip was gone, that he had just been carried out in a body bag, that Laura was shattered, that she said to him,

"I didn't see this coming."

I heard his words, and I was rooted, glued, to the seat of the car, as if stuck on salted ice.

A *body bag*. My heart sank. All the life drained out of *my* body. Images flood my mind.

Trip's beautiful face, eyes full of pain. Things flying in the air around his back yard – flower pots, gardening tools, sticks, leaves, Trip's climbing gear, parts of things he's built – like flocks of birds from the Hitchcock movie. Bijou's soft brown eyes look at me from the back seat.

When I took in what Topper said about Laura not doing well and what she said, I felt angry. How could she not see something coming? They were fighting. She was there. She was closer than I was, and I knew something unhappy was going on.

Topper told me there was a police officer who wanted to talk with me and handed the phone to her. She expressed her sorrow over my loss and told me things I should know, phone numbers, and how to get the autopsy result when it's ready, but she also said she would send emails later. She told me that Laura was in no shape to talk. She was professional but warm. I appreciated that.

Autopsy. What, did they think he's a druggie? Could the autopsy tell me how to live from then on? Could it tell me anything helpful? Why do TV shows and movies always seem to have these scenes from the point of view of the police?

I called my sister Antoinette, the other therapist, and began driving home. She didn't answer. I was just rounding the curve into my neighborhood when Antoinette texted me, "NO NO NO"! Minutes later, she called me and had our sister Betsy on the call, too. We were talking – maddening that *finally,* I had cell service – when the phone rang. It was Joe, my ex, just as I pulled into my garage.

"What in the world"? He asked.

I told him what I knew about the day. When I got to the part about Trip having taken an anti-depressant, he repeated it out loud to Anne, his girlfriend, who is a retired nurse anesthetist. She read from some printed source to Joe that,

"Anti-depressants can sometimes cause people to get suicidal," which he repeated to me.

"Trip took one anti-depressant, and I know from my clinical experience that the chance of that causing him to be suicidal is unlikely," I said, feeling angry. With both Joe and Anne. How dare they start to analyze and speculate? Neither one of them had any idea who Trip really was, even.

"Did Trip have any assets"? Joe asked.

With that, I was stunned. What was he thinking? That he would benefit from the assets if Trip had any? What the hell?

"Why do you ask?" I said. "Oh, I don't know, just wondering," Joe said.

The next day, my two sisters flew out to be with me. I didn't know how I was going to get through the rest of the day or the night until they arrived. I didn't know anything. I didn't remember anything until my sisters showed up at the door, having flown from North Carolina for Betsy and West Virginia for Antoinette. I must have fed Bijou, but I didn't remember doing it.

I believe there is truth and clinical wisdom in the well-known psychiatrist Elizabeth Kubler-Ross's model of the stages of death and dying. They are denial, anger, bargaining, depression, and acceptance. Those stages can happen in cases of loss, death, terminal illness, and other major life-altering changes, either to oneself or to a loved one. Even happy events such as marriage, birth, a new house, or a move can trigger the same responses. Early on, it was thought that they happened in a certain order, but Kubler-Ross later clarified that they might come in any order. Her findings validated what I was feeling. I was in shock and denial; I was angry, just furious. Not at anyone or anything, just angry. I wanted to go back, to stop it all from happening, I wanted to hold on to my memories of my son, his amazing gifts and personality, not have them interrupted by others' inquiries. Shit, I wanted to hold on to my *son.*

The last thing I wanted was someone - anyone – at my door offering casseroles, platitudes, and lots of head-tilting. There was no acceptance in me. I could not imagine making nice and enduring the inevitable, often intrusive, questions about what happened or assuming Trip had a chronic mental illness (he didn't, though he wrote that he often felt abandoned). I didn't want to hear thoughtless and nosy comments that well-meaning people sometimes make.

Of course, I felt like the worst mother ever, guilt oozing out of every pore because I didn't intervene or couldn't stop him. I thought I must be as bad as my pushy, insensitive parents told me I was - or worse. "Stupid, selfish and self-centered" is what my sister Antoinette told me Mother always said to us. I must have stuffed that one way down inside because I didn't remember it. It sounded like her, though. I could picture her saying it as she would be driving me up the roads back home after school. She would have picked me up on the corner where I had been waiting for her, often for as long as 45 minutes. She had us wait at a corner used car lot across from the high school, the corner that was most convenient for her to make the turn back towards home. Driving up the hill, she didn't want to hear from me while she mulled over her own thoughts. Everything was about her.

I tried to sleep. For decades, I had used a technique that I learned in a Fundamentals of Movement class Sophomore year in college. I used it to fall asleep at night. It's that one, now called Body Scan, where you lie on your back and start by focusing on your toes, breathing into them, and getting them to relax. You go up your feet, shins and calves, front and back, doing the same thing, then your knees, front and back, and so on, all the way up your body, part by part, until all of it is relaxed, including your arms, mouth, tongue, eyes, top of your head. It always worked for me, but not then. Images went through my head, and useless thoughts whirred around in the squirrel cage of my mind. Over and over.

At some point, there was a blankness that enveloped me. I breathed but couldn't sleep; I didn't dream or think. My body was on high alert. No rest. In the morning, a voice mail from Trip finally appeared on my phone. It was from the night before he killed himself to tell me what was going on and what he was thinking. About wanting to kill himself because he didn't want to live through a breakup. How he hated to be abandoned. If I had gotten that call when he made it……I don't know if I might have been able to affect his decision. I will never know, but I have an ongoing resentment of AT&T's bad service that night.

What if I had received that call when it was made and been able to talk with him - all night if necessary? What if, AT&T? Damn you,

AT&T. Or, what if I had not gone to the dentist and just talked with Trip? Why didn't I do that? I may never forgive myself for that. I will probably learn to accept it but will live with regret and sadness even still.

Nothing around me looked the same. It looked pale, washed of color and life. My sisters arrived. They looked like themselves: Betsy, slim, blonde, wearing her clothes well, standing the same way she did as a little girl, feet planted, with knees that almost go backward. She was the tallest one, the one Mother said was pretty. Antoinette, dark hair with a teensy bit of gray in it, big deep-blue eyes, as pretty as Betsy, just different. She and I believed neither of us was the pretty one. Mother had told us so often about Betsy being pretty that we still believed her. Betsy was built more like mother and was mother's favorite. Not that Betsy ever felt it much because of how Mother was. Antoinette has daddy's good looks and smile. I'm a mix, a mutt, the one whose looks were never good enough for mother. My feet were too flat, my lips too full. I was too short and weighed too much. She was always finding something wrong with me. Antoinette was the one my kids called "Auntoinette" distinguishing her from their sister Antoinette. That was Trip's idea. Betsy and Antoinette were a relief from the pain that day. I was grateful for them. I had no idea what I looked like. I didn't feel like a solid mass. More like scattered pieces of skin and bone and something else I couldn't name. Topper said *body bag.*

My sisters were barely in the door when my phone rang. I was upstairs when it did. It was a woman I know. I didn't answer. I didn't want to talk. I didn't want to *listen.* I sure as heck didn't want the head tilting with its looks of pity. Within minutes, the doorbell rang, the door opened and in walked the very same woman who had just called on the phone. She was loudly calling out my name while walking into my house. How dare she? I signaled "NO" to my sisters who, with kindness - kindness not in me at the moment - sent the caller away. How did she even *know,* I wondered? Later, I remembered that I had called Betsy, my best friend in Colorado, and told her. She was in the hospital in Denver for a knee replacement. She, being a bit out of it from surgery, must have forgotten I wanted to keep it quiet for a day or so and told her sister, who was out of the country. Her sister, also a friend of mine, told the people she was with. This is a small community, and it doesn't take any time for word to spread. I knew that and had wanted to avoid it happening until I got out of town.

———

I remember being five years old and playing with my kid-sized metal fire engine. I made up a story that there was a big fire, jumped into the little fire engine, and slammed my foot down on one of the pedals when my foot slipped, cutting my ankle right to the bone. Mother threatened to punish me if I cried when she took me to old Doc Davis, my grandfather's friend. He used staples to close the wound. She told me she wouldn't take me to see Santa Claus if I cried. I didn't. It has been a strong inhibition of mine ever since.

———

My tears were still deep inside, gnawing. I wished they would come out, but I was paralyzed by the grief, horror, and finality of this loss. I kept feeling as if Trip's suicide was my fault, my shame. Part of the shame was that back in my youth, the Catholic Church taught that suicide was wrong, a going-to-hell sin against God. Maybe it still teaches that. I resented that dogma. I don't believe it and many other things I was taught, but there it was, within me, glued to my bones and rearing its ugly head, this unforgiving, unkind, farthest-thing-from-compassion dogma. The worst thing was that he was gone. I still can't take that in.

I love Vail and the Rocky Mountains and have easily made them my home. I'll be riding a bike (road bike and sometimes a mountain bike), playing tennis, doing short, steep hikes, and working to improve my skiing until my last day. I enjoy it all. All of that and continuing to get to know and love me. That's the constant rub – continuing to shed the person my parents told me I was and becoming me. It is a difficult task. My parents shamed and thwarted the real me from the time I was born. I became reticent about myself– who I am, how I feel about myself, my opinions, ideas, dreams, thoughts, and some things that have happened to me. I have spent much of my life trying to emerge from the sick psychological cocoon of my parents and to fly with my own wings. I believed I was bad, unlovable, and unworthy. I developed a habit of hiding from my parents, most authority figures, even my friends, and, in many ways, myself. I was afraid to be known.

My parents were overbearing and narcissistic alcoholics who were poster people for the rigid patriarchal era that is only now starting to give way to a new age. They didn't love my two sisters or me. They cowed and belittled me enough to make me want to run away from home. When I was young, the problem was, where would I go? My sisters say they had the same problem: wanting to go but not knowing where.

By all outward appearances, we had a good and privileged life. We always had a nice home, enough food, access to good health care and education. My first memories are of my maternal grandparents' loving and gracious home. We were there during World War II because my father expected to be called up for military service at any time. I was told later that he didn't want to leave infant me and mother in our little house that had an unreliable gas furnace. After my grandparents', we moved to our own home, where we lived when my sisters were born. When I was starting seventh grade, we moved to a larger, even more comfortable home on a ridge top seven miles outside of the city where we lived, Charleston, West Virginia. There, we had two equines – a horse for my father and a pony for me, and often a third horse that belonged to friends who boarded their horse with us. We had a small horse barn, two pastures, and lots of wooded hillside that went down to a creek. I can still conjure up the aroma of the surrounding forested hills and the rich green of the landscape. Instead of see-forever views, the hills gave glimpses of more, of native dogwoods, mountain laurel, and rhododendron, sounds of life from across the hills. There was a tennis club on one of the other hills. In summer, with the windows open, we could hear the distant thwack of tennis balls being hit. I feel a sense of peace and of being held by the natural world when I recall those memories. The state is vertical and beautifully clothed by nature.

Chapter Two

I don't believe that old Catholic dogma about suicide. I was haunted by the idea and stigma of it. I wanted Trip to show me that he was in a good place just to prove the dogma wrong. That he was surrounded by love.

I knew he was in a good place because of an experience I had had decades before. I was 39 years old. It was a month or two after Mother had called me (from three hundred miles away in West Virginia) to say while laying on her kitchen floor, that she couldn't take it anymore. She had taken a bunch of pills and washed them down with wine. In spite of herself, she was rescued and lived a long life of denial about her alcoholism and continuing co-dependence on my father, also an alcoholic.

The wine and pill experience did not change Mother, but it was a turning point for me. I had been unhappy in my lonely marriage, in pain from having my parents off the rails in so many ways, and as the mother of five beautiful teenagers who needed guidance and love, I was stretched and flailing. I thought all of it was my responsibility, my fault. Not only did both parents not love us, but their treatment of us was and had been controlling and inhibiting. Mother told me once that what she learned in a class on early childhood education was that the best way to get a child to obey you was to shame him or her. Not long after mother's meltdown, I was driving east into Richmond, Virginia, on US Rt 6/Patterson Ave. when the traffic light at Pump Rd turned red. As I came to a stop, a clear, strong voice in my head said to me,

"It's not your fault".

I saw as if in a movie, images of the *interconnectedness of Everything*: past, present, future, and many universes in the vast realms of space. And what I understood at that moment was that the thing that held it all together was love. Love. I burst into tears as my heart opened to everything, including me. Even me. I lived in a bubble of compassion, love, and acceptance for the next many months until the newness of it subsided. It had infiltrated my being, though, and the meaning of it has gradually sunk in, and little by little has been transforming me ever since. Leonard Cohen wrote in Anthem, "every heart, every heart, to love will come". I am grateful to Trip for being the one who introduced me to Leonard Cohen. What I needed, and perhaps most of us need, is a healthy love for our own selves.

At the time, I came to think and feel differently about people I found hard to take for all different reasons. Some seemed to think they were above the rest of us. Some annoyed me because they were bent on being so correct about everything or thinking that their way was the correct way. Some just plain got under my skin. After the Pump and Patterson moment, I looked at those people and realized that they were doing their best. One of those people was a man, the anesthesiologist, who didn't believe me when I said I could feel the knife cutting me open during my second set of twins' birth by C-section. He turned to his assistant and said, "Oh, these women, they think they feel things, but they really don't." He couldn't accept that the epidural he gave me might have been a hair or two off the mark. Proud man. I made him promise to knock me out when it was time for me to be stitched back together. He did.

The result of that experience at the stoplight was that I *knew* there was, and is, so much love and goodness to go around - a deep, unending well of it. But it's now that I know that. I didn't for the many years before. Didn't begin to until that moment at Pump and Patterson. The memory of the other is painful. And to think that I had been raising my children in that same stew where love was in short supply. I didn't mean to, but I had been swimming in it my whole life and didn't know any different.

———

I kept asking Trip to please show me – prove to me that what I knew was true, that he was in a good place, a loving place. One morning, he did show me. He appeared just as I was waking. His spirit was standing there in jeans and a T-shirt, blue eyes twinkling at me as if he was greeting me with his familiar "Hi, Mom" in his resonant voice. He had a wide white bandage around his head. Someone had cared for him. It covered most of his head of dark, curly hair. I was overjoyed to see him, to feel his presence. It relieved my heart to know that he heard me and that he looked quite content. He was radiating love. It didn't take away the pain of his loss. It didn't keep me from wanting to wish away this whole episode and bring Trip back.

Feeling as desperate and lost as I did, I needed to connect with my four daughters - Dana in Idaho and the other three in Virginia: Antoinette, Kate, and Carter - about getting together. We decided when and where we should meet. It was going to be at Antoinette's house - daughter Antoinette. I had a need to see them, talk with them, and think of some way to remember Trip, to celebrate who he was and his life.

I was dying to talk with Laura, too, but she hadn't been up to it. She and Trip had been together for the past five years. Tall and blond, Laura was the mother of three daughters, two in college and one just beginning high school. She had been divorced since before she and Trip were an item. Trip represented adventure; she once told me. She had been, at least until recently, quite taken with him. When she did call, I was in my dining room with my sisters. I got up and started walking around the table with the phone to my ear. What I said, I can't recall exactly. I know I exclaimed to Laura that I was glad she called, and I asked her how she was.

She told me how things went for her that day. I'm paraphrasing when I say what I remember. Trip called her at work to tell her what he was thinking of doing. She panicked and planned to drive home. At some point, one of the neighbors called to tell her that Trip was walking around with a gun in his hand, saying, 'I won't be committed.' (I am pretty sure that comment related to the problem Laura's daughter had during the past summer over the break-up with *her* boyfriend. He had made a failed attempt to end his life. She got so upset that Laura and Trip had her committed for her to get some help and not hurt herself.) When Laura got home, Trip still had the gun in his hand. She fought with him to take it away just as a police car drove up – one of the neighbors had called them. When she went to talk to the policeman, Trip went into the backyard and shot himself. By this time, Laura and I were both in tears. Mine surprised me, coming in sobs and gulps completely out of my control. We start talking about what we love about Trip. "He was so creative, so intuitive," I said. She agreed.

That's when she told me that Trip had been sitting in front of his computer every day, just staring at the screen for a long time - more than a week, maybe two or three? And he hadn't been sleeping at all. I didn't know any of that. I wished she had told me before. If she had, I would have known that it was depression, and maybe I could have made a difference. Lack of sleep contributes a lot toward causing depression. He wasn't chronically depressed. This was a situational depression. But he always expected a lot of himself and often, he was intense about meeting his own expectations.

I knew that he and Laura had argued when Trip had been here at my house in July. One day, I heard his raised voice while he was talking with her on the phone. That was when Trip, Dana, and Antoinette were here for several days of pure fun with the four of us - hiking, playing tennis, and taking a float trip on the Colorado River. Looking back, Trip could have already been checking out of life or thinking about it because he orchestrated the float trip and paid for it. Before that, he asked me one day if I had done that kind of trip on the Colorado River. I had not. (What I had done was a very active paddle trip down the Colorado through the Grand Canyon, but not this relaxed float trip on the Upper Colorado). I think that he wanted to provide that for me. The kids' visit was four days of fun, except there was one afternoon when some loud words came from Trip through the door of his room. It was clear that he was talking with Laura. I don't know what it was about, but it was loud.

He had told me prior to this visit that Laura was very worried about her daughter with the ex-boyfriend and blaming herself for the daughter's troubles. I know Trip had been trying to help Laura not blame herself, but things between them must have eroded. Later, after his phone call with Laura, "Mom, mom, mom!" said Trip.

He walked toward me, distressed, sounding like a young kid looking for a hug, a mom hug. I turned and said "Trip" as I hugged him. Antoinette and Dana looked surprised at his needy gesture.

After the girls flew home, Trip and I were sitting on my deck on a Colorado blue sky day, just lazing about. That's when he told me about Laura and that they were fighting. That she wasn't *the one.* I remembered how he had been over his marriage break-up but told myself the same thing I did a couple of days ago, that he was older and knew that life goes on. I had learned denial at my mother's knee. It's what she did with reality because she wasn't into any kind of self-awareness. I had often been afraid to speak the truth, even to myself. To let myself in on the truth of how I felt about myself: flawed and unlovable. By the time I was in grad school, I had let myself in on that one. But when Trip was right in front of me in such distress, such danger, I reverted to old habits.

I used to say to myself before my grandparents died that I'd never lost anyone close to me. That I was lucky that way. When my grandparents and parents died, they had lived full lives, and it was in the natural order of things. Trip killing himself was not in the natural order. I felt terrible, a bad person, unworthy of anything good – the things that Mother used to tell me. I thought that all my efforts to heal and be whole – starting with the stoplight revelation and what followed, including a long period of healing after divorce, had evaporated. I felt as if they never happened or they didn't amount to much.

Before that, just a few months before, I had been asking myself about my purpose at that stage in life. Should I have kept working as a therapist? Do something different? I had been seeing clients, learning to ski better, participating in my community here, and socializing with friends, many of them already retired. I had been wondering what would give meaning to my life for this last third of it.

Missing him with everything in me, my mind drifted to memories of Trip. He was four when I drove him the three blocks to St. Christopher's School for him to be interviewed for a spot in the kindergarten class. I had dressed him in his best outfit and tried to seem casual about him going to see a person who would be asking him questions about himself. The interviewer, a lower-school teacher, probed him for awareness of his world. Little had escaped his notice.

"5908 Kensington Avenue," he had said when asked where he lived.

Next, she had asked him to show her how he brushed his teeth, to see if he was right or left

handed. He was left-handed, but the teacher didn't find out that day.

"I already brushed my teeth today. They don't need brushing now."

"Well, just pretend," she prodded.

"I don't need to brush my teeth."

"Do you have any brothers or sisters at home?"

"Four sisters."

"Are they older than you or younger than you?"

"Younger."

She knew that couldn't be right. She saw from the paperwork that Trip was four.

"Are you sure about that, Trip?"

"Yes," he had said.

"They're all younger sisters?" she asked again, incredulous.

"Yes."

She asked several times, and each time, Trip assured her that he had four younger sisters.

Then the light dawned. After the interview, the teacher told me that she had heard about us from someone she knew. We lived on a street that bordered part of the school. It was true. At age four, Trip *did* have four younger sisters.

———

My adult life was built around the family that started with Trip. Not intentionally, but because he happened. I was out of college by then and teaching in a high school. Talk about shame. Every mother in my generation told her daughters, "Don't. Get. Pregnant." That was the first and most important commandment. If you were raised Catholic, the commandment was even more important. It was right up there with Don't Use Birth Control. What a "Catch 22" that was! My mother added the admonition that I was not allowed to go steady because girls who went steady got pregnant. I didn't go steady. Worthless advice. I'm pretty sure she was thinking of high school when she said that. I was in high school then. I didn't think it meant don't date during and after college. But when Joe and I became sexually active – after college - I should have had the nerve to get a prescription for the birth control pill. I didn't. I didn't want to be shamed or embarrassed by some strange doctor. Planned Parenthood didn't exist yet. Yet how can I berate myself when we had such great kids? Even if I do say so myself.

My parents were difficult and traumatic to have as parents. My father ran a wholesale business that his father had started. My mother ran our home with the help of a woman, Annie, who lived at our house except for her days off, Thursdays and every other weekend. Mother had a regular bridge game, was a member of a garden club, though she was not a gardener – she employed a gardener (Annie's husband, Sam) - and did some volunteer work as a member of the Junior League. That's the way it was in her generation and social group. She was invested in and presided over what we three daughters chose for our activities outside of school. When Betsy wanted shoe skates for roller or ice skating, I was not allowed to have them, too. I had a pony. Antoinette did ballet and tennis. I'm not sure why mother felt she had to control us in that way. Did she not want us to compete the way she did with her own brother? She was competitive with her brother, her children, and probably her mother. She was critical of her mother's looks, taste, and other things about her – the way she pronounced "push." It sounded too West Virginian, too hillbilly, to suit mother. Never mind that mother was born, raised, and lived her whole life in West Virginia. She did, however, go to a boarding school for a year or two. After that, she put herself on a pedestal and looked down on many others. She failed to recognize the warm and good human being her mother was. She wanted *all* her father's affection and attention. She wanted all of whatever she valued. Her mother, the grandmother we called Nana, asked me several times during her life why my mother was "like that," which I think meant judgmental and haughty. Whatever the name, it hurt Nana, and she didn't understand it. It felt shaming to me. Shaming about every sphere of my life, especially my looks, body shape, size, and lacking many capabilities that she thought I should have. Mother was about 5'6" with long, slim arms and legs. Her ideal was the comment attributed to Wallis Simpson and others: "No woman can be too rich or too thin." My feet were too flat (a sign of being not well-bred, according to her), and my lips too fat – I don't know the reason on that one. Then out of the blue one day, she exclaimed, "your hands! They look just like a man!" Because my veins stood out. Maybe because I had muscles and mother didn't. She wanted me/us to excel in sports, academics, artwork, and, most of all, how we appeared to others. We were supposed to conform to her social expectations: perfect manners, refined looks – if we had been horses, the term for the looks would have been "good conformation."

My parents had become less and less physically active in each decade. They had played social tennis and golf when I was young, and my father rode horses for years before I was born and then for a few of the same years that I also did between grade school and college. When they were in their 40s, they gave up such activities for nothing but their regular cocktails daily. They didn't even take walks! They did allow my sisters and me to learn swimming and tennis and we even got lessons in those things along with piano or art classes – ballet for Antoinette. Like I said, mother presided over all of it. My father grumbled - loudly - about the cost of everything.

My salvation was horses. My relationships with them were how I experienced love. My father had ridden as a young man, both foxhunting and showing horses whose owners could not or did not. He was a proficient enough rider that other people asked him to ride their open jumper horses in horse shows for them. He had a small trophy collection. When he read Anna Sewell's book, Black Beauty, to me on Christmas Day when I was six or so, I was hooked. Horses became my heart connection. As were many of my pets –guppies, a rabbit, a few cats, more than one dog, all the tadpoles I could catch (I turned them loose when they became frogs), a parakeet - I was allowed to have until Mother got tired of them. I gave them all names. The parakeet was Honey. I'd say, "Hi Honey," and she'd say "Hi Honey" back to me.

Daddy liked to bird hunt, and for years he had dogs, Pointers, for finding and retrieving quail. The first one we called Brown Mac – he was brown and white. He was with us at my maternal grandparents' when we lived there during the war. After Brown Mac, the second dog we called Black Mac. He was black and white. "Why is he called Mac, too?" I asked. Daddy said, "The trainer names all the dogs Mac." I assume that means they were all male. Like so many men, neither he nor my father or his father wanted female dogs back then. In the case of horses, no mares, either. Interesting how male superiority and Patriarchy even include pet animals. The dogs weren't allowed in our house. They were chained to a doghouse outside. However, Brown Mac was allowed to accompany me on walks to my friend Mimi's house back when we lived with my grandparents. I yearned for a pet dog who would be allowed in the house, like Mimi's dog. We had one, briefly, when I was four. She was a cocker spaniel, but she had to stay in the garage and squealed every time the door went up or down. Because of her squealing, she wasn't there long enough for me to get to know her. A few years later, mother bought a puppy she saw in a store window. I named her Cricket. She was sweet and soft. She hadn't been there very long when mother ran over her while backing the car out one day. I saw the car go over her, shrieked, "Puppy!" and held her for her last moments as she bit me in her pain. Mother kept going.

We finally got another pet dog, Jado, when I was 12. He was a three-year-old show dog, a Boxer, given to us by friends of my parents who were getting a different breed. He was a special friend – slept on my bed (against the rules) and went horseback riding with me on all the trails. He was allowed in the house, a first, was a great family dog and very playful, like most Boxers. He wasn't at all pugilistic. Instead, if another dog approached him looking for a fight when we were out on a trail, Jado would sit down on his haunches with his tongue sticking out in the way that only Boxers can do, looking very nonchalant. It was his way of saying 'no thank you.' He wasn't into fighting. It worked.

My job from age four until college was to feed the dogs every single day. After we moved out to the ridgetop, I also fed the horses twice a day, turned them out in the pasture, and mucked out their stalls. That was supposed to teach me to be responsible. My parents didn't understand that I *loved* the horses and dogs and taking care of them and that I was born responsible. The awful part was being interrogated daily to make sure I had done my job. After my husband, Joe, and I had our son and four daughters, mother asked me one day, "Did having the dog and horse responsibilities make it easier to manage all these children?" I was stunned by her assumption and self-congratulation and almost gagged.

 I wasn't allowed to go to the college I wanted, where I had been accepted (Sophie Newcomb, which is now part of Tulane) or to follow the dreams for myself that went with that beginning. Neither one of them wanted me to go far from home. Of course, I hadn't told them much about my dreams because I didn't trust them to resist shaming me about them. They even told me what I should do after I graduated. By then, I'd given up any of my own dreams. If I could have been brave enough to create a T-shirt back in my youth, I think it might have said, "Stop telling me who you think I am."

It's ironic that mother always assumed that I would be back in town to live after college. The truth was that I couldn't wait to *leave* town because of her and my father. Mother had assumed from the time I was two years old that I was her designated caretaker. It started one day when she was in pain from what turned out to be an ectopic pregnancy. When the phone rang, mother was too ill to get up to answer it and told me to pick up the phone and tell the caller to please come help, that mother was sick. The caller was Nana, my grandmother, whose home we were living in at the time. Mother was rushed to the hospital and survived what could have been a fatal event. Mother expected such attendance from me forever more. My sister Antoinette tells me that she felt the same expectation was placed on her.

I married the boy, Joe, whom I dated after college because we got pregnant, and I didn't want to be an unwed mother. I kept that a secret from everyone else until it became obvious. Joe had floated the idea of abortion, but I already had a relationship with the little person inside me, the one who turned out to be Trip. After that, I tried to live the fairy tale of happy ever after. That didn't work out so well, but I loved being a mom and loved our kids. What I didn't know then or for years was that I didn't love myself. Not having been loved by my parents, I hadn't learned to love myself.

The first good part was having Trip, and then, I wanted to have more kids because I loved him, thought he was adorable and the best thing I'd done so far. I had always wanted to be a mom. That led to the next good part, if a bit unorthodox, having two sets of twin girls in rather rapid succession. It could have been less rapid, but it was all good. Just quick. Twins had not been in either family. The first two arrived when Trip was 27 months old, and the next two when he was three and five months old. We'd been married 3 years when the last set was born. I was a successful broodmare.

The first set of twin girls, named Antoinette and Kate, were fraternal twins, and they looked it. Antoinette had blond hair and green eyes. Kate had dark brown eyes and brown hair. The second set of girls, Carter and Dana, were identical, with brown hair and blue eyes. The wonderful thing about them all is that each one was his or her own person, pretty much from the get-go. If there was anything I had hoped for my kids, it was that very thing, the freedom to be who they were, not anything prescribed by someone else – especially me or their father. That was a reaction to my own upbringing, a reaction I still believe is a good thing.

The marriage didn't take in large part because I married an alcoholic whose main relationship was with his drink of choice. Children of alcoholics often unconsciously choose an alcoholic spouse. I am no exception. Joe wasn't overbearing like my parents but was emotionally unavailable and oblivious to emotional cues or needs. We stayed together for 29 years, raising kids and living in the country with the kids all on horseback for some part of that time. I had to talk Joe into the country because he was a city boy, born and raised in Richmond, Virginia. He had spent a lot of time on the rivers east of Richmond, ones that fed into the Chesapeake Bay. Boats, water, and guns for hunting were much more to his liking than horses, pastures, and tractors.

We bought part of an old farm, the part with the house that was built in 1900. It was a former dairy farm (the cows were gone) where we raised kids, horses, cats, dogs, some laying hens, Antoinette's guinea pig or two (they gnawed a hole and escaped into the space in the walls), and a big garden in an as yet-un-suburbanized area in the red clay dirt piedmont west of Richmond.

In West Virginia, I learned to love and ride horses. The same place where I learned to appreciate the "wild and wonderful" hills and the good and independent people there. "Mountaineers are always Free" is the state motto. I know West Virginia has been the butt of tons of jokes, and the people have been subjected to the needs of huge fossil fuel and chemical corporations that have not enhanced their lives or education. The consequence is that their standard of living has been lower because of it. Graft and corruption have been rampant. Nevertheless, it is a naturally beautiful state with some beautiful people, and it deserves better than to be fodder for jokes.

I went to college in Virginia because my parents went there for a party/steeplechase weekend and came back having enrolled me in a college I had never even heard of, let alone considered. That's how I wound up in Virginia. At the time, I felt as if my parents were always managing me. They were. Now I wonder, did they do it because they thought I was incapable? They were still doing it when I had finished school and was interviewing for teaching positions. I had an offer in Atlanta, which at the time was sort of the New York of the South. It was a popular place for college grads. My father pooh-poohed that plan, saying, "No, you'll get a job, and then the schools will close." That would have been because integration of the schools was just beginning and there was lots of resistance to that in the south. He had also said New Orleans and Sophie Newcomb were too far away.

In hindsight, I can see that the country part of married life is what kept me sane. I loved it. The kids, the animals, mucking stalls, the gardening, the chaos of so many kids so close in age. I had time to reflect as I rode a horse and drove a tractor to mow the pastures – in the local language, no one said "mow"; they said "bush hog," as in I bush-hogged the pasture - or because the kids went to school in Richmond, I drove back and forth the twenty-some miles to town. I drove so many round trips to town that I told Joe when I died; he could just spread my ashes on Rt 6, the road to town. He usually drove the kids to school in the morning when he was going to work, but after-school activities were my responsibility.

What I didn't have, that I'd never had was another adult who loved and/or encouraged me and who had my back. No, that's not quite true. I can't put my maternal grandparents in that group. They did love their children and grandchildren and thought we were all very special. They were special, too. In part because they loved each other very much and took care of themselves. They walked two miles every morning before breakfast and two miles after dinner each evening. They played tennis and golf together and traveled far and wide. They lived long, healthy, and productive lives in love with each other to the end. Nana lived until a few months before her 91st birthday.

I was always doubting myself, not asking questions, looking for something, or someone, somewhere, to tell me that I was an ok person. And keeping myself to myself. I still have to learn how to let myself be known a little more. To be less guarded. If I had not had a dream that told me so and an analyst who highlighted it, I might not have noticed that about myself, that I have been hiding my real self for most of my life. It comes naturally as a therapist to draw out others, not so much for oneself. In the dream, I was lying in a bed with a handsome man who was naked. I was saying to him, "If I'd known you would be naked, I would have gotten naked, too."

As I look back and mull it over, I see I did have courage and was not a conformist, the nothing person my parents thought I was, but I did not know how to embrace the strong me for the first 50 years or more. My two younger sisters are good people who weathered the same parents, but for a long time, we each made do in our own way. That is often the way in dysfunctional families. As we got older, we collaborated and were sisters who loved each other.

Because of the family that Joe and I began, I left my parents, which was a psychologically healthy thing, but it was only a physical leaving for several years. Even though Joe and I got married and lived 300 miles away from my parents, my parents were still very much in my head and my psyche. I told myself that if Joe and I loved each other, then it would be ok, and so would I. But instead of learning to love each other, we grew apart. It wasn't physically apart, but we weren't close, either. Sort of parallel tracks with very little discussion. Some of that may well have been my habit of keeping to myself. He did his thing, and I did my thing. It wasn't ok, and neither was I. The cloud of shame and fear were still with me, but I ignored it for a long time because there were the kids. I loved them and had always wanted to be a mom.

It didn't take Joe long after our marriage to start overdoing his alcohol intake and coming home late and drunk. Before we married, when he said to me, "I don't want to have a drink every night." I thought that meant that he already knew he had a problem and was just going to manage it. I just didn't want to know that. Denial was my best suit. I learned it from my parents, who did it daily, pretending that they were just fine; thank you very much, and all was well. And Joe was good at concealing his intake at first.

As for my parents being just fine, they weren't. The resentment and anger they carried toward each other and each other's families was close enough to the surface that I was aware of it at a very young age. There were also their raging arguments that became physical.

Maybe that's why it took three years or more for me to accept what was happening to Joe and me, and by then, we were deep in diapers.

———

When Trip was a toddler, I was besotted with him. I'll never forget the day that he was sitting on a little yellow wooden giraffe with wheels, a blue baby bib on his head with a straw sombrero on top of that, and grinning his happy, aren't-I-funny grin, I said to myself:

"He is so cute. We have to do this again."

That bit of my life was extreme, I know, but I wanted to be a mom. I see in hindsight that I grabbed the opportunity when it presented itself. I'm convinced that I wanted to be the mother I never had. I wanted four kids because, as a kid, I thought my first cousins had so much more fun as a foursome. Nevertheless, it was double, triple – pun intended – fun most of the time, at least for me. After his death, Trip showed me that he was in a loving place.

Chapter Three

I was told that I was premature (4lbs, 10oz.) and that's why I was skinny – which may be true, but not 2.5 months true. I never did the math and never noticed I was born only 6.5 months after my parents married until my mom told me in my late 30s (recently). [this is hyperbole. I did not wait until he was that old!]

25 Random Things About Me #1, Trip Lucas, Facebook.

In a day or two, I called Topper again because the police wanted to know where Trip's body should go and what funeral home. Topper gave me the name of the only one in Austin that he was somewhat familiar with. I called them and arranged for Trip's body to go there for him to be cremated. They wanted me to pick up his effects and his remains when ready. His *remains*. I said I would call back. I was making these decisions about my son, for god's sake. It was really happening. I was numb but functioning at the same time. I fluctuated between furious and frozen, between overwhelmed and empty. I wanted to cry more, but the tears didn't come. The worst thing I could possibly imagine had happened, and after, I couldn't cry. Again.

I had decided that I would go to Virginia on Sunday to meet with Joe and our daughters. That would be the fourth day since Trip's death. Early that Sunday, Auntoinette and I took Bijou to the home of the woman, Anne, who used to dog-sit for me. She lost her son to suicide when he was 20, over a break-up. I was acutely aware of that but had thought of nothing to say to her.

She said to me, "I'm so sorry. This is a club no one wants to belong to." No kidding, I was thinking, and how ironic, but I was still in such shock that I said very little in reply to her. Not anything even resembling joining her in her experience of loss. I was too numb. I knew I didn't want to leave little Bijou with her. It was as if the puppy had then taken the place of Trip. She was my child, and I worried about her being traumatized by being suddenly left at that place that she'd never seen before. I was lonely for her before I even left her.

My sisters and I drove two cars to the airport in Denver. Auntoinette drove the rental, and Betsy rode with me. I wished we could have all been together in the same car. I wanted them both near me. At the time, I was growing more and more separated from my body, from my sense of the present, as if twirling in the air, a leaf. "This can't be happening," I must have been thinking.

Looking back, I don't remember which airport I flew into in Virginia. I didn't remember if someone met me or if I got a car. I remembered that Kim, Trip's ex-wife, had called. She mentioned how distraught her father was over Trip and that he wanted me to call him. Betsy was sitting in the Denver airport with me when I called him. He had been like a father to Trip. A soft-spoken man, he was a good woodworker and all-around handy man. He taught Trip a lot of what he knew about those things and Trip had consulted him often. Kim said that her father was always amazed at how Trip could decide he wanted to learn something and then do it. It warmed my heart to hear that. That's the Trip I knew.

I don't remember when I told Joe, my ex, that I did not want his girlfriend, Anne, to meet with us that first day when we would be gathered to talk about Trip and how to proceed. He said,

"Oh, she's very sensitive about these things, and she's nice to our girls."

"Anne has seen Trip two times that I know of. She didn't raise him, and I don't care how sensitive she is; I don't want her there", I said, having found my backbone and a willingness to open my mouth and speak for myself.

It was a warm day when we all assembled at Antoinette's. Like most nights since it happened, I had slept little, if at all. I had lost flesh off my body. My clothes were falling off me, and it had only been five days. In the photos, I looked like a kid playing dress-up. Maybe I will blow away, I thought. Right then, I'd have liked that. I didn't know how I'd survive. On the screened porch, looking out at the pool, at Antoinette's two dogs, the green, plant-surrounded and fenced backyard looked the same yet strange, too. It might as well have been Mars. Antoinette is my Olympic athlete daughter. She was on the U.S. field hockey team for twelve years, during which the team played in the '96 Olympics. After that, she coached at a local university for another 12 years. Like the rest of my daughters and Trip, she was active and quite an athlete.

Joe showed up, nodding his head up and down over and over as he strode toward me. What does that mean? I wondered. It felt sort of grandiose or smug, like "I told you so," or "Well, you've really done it now." I wanted to slap him. Why didn't he say something, damn it? Something comforting or caring? Or connecting? He was grayer, looked older, stiffer than when I had last seen him. Or maybe he had been that way before? My daughter Carter arrived with her husband, Alan, and my grandson, Sandy. Carter was the one who finished high school a year early (expertly convincing her school to allow it) and spent that year with a family in Norway. She was living out the prophecy of her Collegiate School teachers had uttered about her: "Life for Carter will always be an exploration." Alan and Sandy left for work and school after saying hello, so sorry, hugs. Everything – or maybe it's just me – felt sort of stilted. The rest of us, Joe, our four girls, Antoinette, Kate, Carter, Dana, and I, sat down at a table on the deck, the deck that Trip had built for Antoinette. It connected the space between the screened porch and the hot tub. Building it was so Trip - he pretty much learned to do things by doing them. Like Kim's dad said about Trip, deciding he wanted to learn something and then doing it.

First, someone asked when and where we might do a memorial service.

"I don't think we need to do any kind of service or anything," Joe says.

I was stunned. I breathed in and out. I wondered if he still believed those Catholic teachings. Was he angry with Trip? What the hell? He and Trip hadn't been close. Joe had never been to see Trip in any of the many places he lived, worked, or learned, but really? I didn't ask or say anything. What would have been the point? Anyway, I didn't care what Joe thought about a service. I knew what I wanted to do. Lots of ideas were passed around.

"I'll be leaving for Maui in two weeks," Kate said. Since she owns a business that puts on triathlons and races, she feels she needs to go for business reasons but also to compete. She had qualified for the Xterra World Championship in Maui. It's a big deal to qualify and compete in the World Championship.

Someone said maybe we could have a service before then.

"No way. I can't be ready this week or next for a service. I just can't. Where would we even have it?" I said.

We no longer lived near each other, and none of us were affiliated with a church or religion now. We used to be. At that time, I was still recovering from being dogmatized by Catholicism, a dogmatism that precluded the possibility of the revelation of anything new. Joe said he was a recovering alcoholic. Finally, I thought our kids were in very different spaces regarding church and religion. None of them were affiliated. Trip seemed to have been the only one that had given it much thought at that point. Of course, he had matriculated from an Episcopalian school before college. He was outspoken about what he thought in his 25 Random Things About Me, that I discovered on his Facebook page. The kids had been baptized Catholic, but when it came time to prepare Trip for his first Holy Communion, I couldn't stomach the parents' guide, and Joe didn't even discuss it, or anything else, with me.

My phone rang. It was the funeral home in Austin. The man on the phone was practiced and a teensy bit unctuous. Topper said *body bag*. The funeral home man says *Cremation. Remains.* I had with me the papers to sign for the cremation. Joe pulled out his checkbook and wrote me a check for half. That surprised me partly because he had told me he didn't have any money when we divorced, insisting that he wasn't lying to me about that, and partly because I thought, based on his comments, that he wasn't going to have anything to do with whatever happened regarding Trip. I wonder if, because cremation is not a memorial service, he was willing to share the expense.

I wanted to run somewhere, but there is a part of me that puts one foot in front of the other, the part that doesn't collapse until it is all over. The part that takes injured or sick kids and animals to the hospital when they get hurt, no matter how worried I am. The part that kept going. Even then. When you are the mom and married to an emotionally disconnected alcoholic, you have to be the engine. The motor. The starter. Or something – one of those things.

I know that's a contradiction to the mute me with no voice, but I could see since I'd been writing that all along, there was a knowing me or a courageous me who continued to develop in spite of the constant parental assaults. Maybe it was a silently rebellious me. The part that refused to tell on seven-year-old me when mother asked me one night at dinner to tell my father what I had done that day. I was the only one at the dinner table with my parents for several years until my sisters were old enough to join us. That was a fish-bowl set-up. I could never hide unwanted food in my napkin or get away with anything the least bit naughty. What I had done that day was go to the fish-pond next door. My father had forbidden me to *ever* go to the neighbor's pond. But that day, I went anyway. It was just too intriguing with the fish swimming around and frogs sitting on the edge looking for bugs and flies, and the croaking. The croaking was a genuine delight. I suppose I had read stories and heard about frogs croaking but had never heard the croaking before. The pond was in a green, alluring, and lively place nestled into the wooded hillside on the other side of the picket fence between us and our neighbors. The neighbors, the Davises, were nice and friends of my grandparents. That night at dinner, I must have decided that not telling on myself would be less awful than having Daddy (whose temper frightened the life out of me) punish me for going to the forbidden place. Instead, he was so furious for my not telling that he picked me up by both shoulders, marched me upstairs to my room, and slammed me down on my bed hard enough that I imagined I might bounce up and hit the glow-in-the-dark stars that were stuck to the ceiling. What, I wonder now, was Mother's reason for even bringing up my infraction? For throwing me under the bus?

That seems to be the same part of me, the not telling part, that puts one foot in front of the other. The hard part was not having anyone to talk with about how I was feeling, how everyone was feeling, and what to do next. I had no shoulder to lean on, and I was still holding my breath after Trip's death. I had a yawning, aching hole inside of me. Yet, here was that scared but silent little rebel, as well. I think she says, "Don't you dare tell me what to do."

We dispersed, with the place and the date of any celebration of Trip's life still undecided. Kate and I talked about finding a place for the service and were thinking about the University of Virginia chapel. Trip graduated from the University of Virginia.

We left Antoinette's and drove over to Charlottesville, where Kate lived, to look at the UVA chapel, the Gothic stone chapel that doesn't look a thing like the rest of the University with its red brick Jeffersonian style and its rotunda. We were there just before a wedding took place. I froze and wanted to throw up at the same time. I couldn't stomach why I was there. Kate drove around this part of Charlottesville as we talked.

"If only I could have kept him talking," Kate said.

I must have left after that, but again, there was a blank in my memory about the travel details. I went back to Colorado, but from which airport? How? I was lost in space, untethered to anything in me that felt solid. And after, I didn't remember. I think I must have flown from Charlottesville, where Kate lived. It would make sense, but I had no memory of doing that or anything else.

At home, I started making phone calls to the University of Virginia chapel in order to reserve it for Trip's memorial and got frustrated with the bureaucracy and insensitivity of the process. I kept being told that the person in charge was unavailable or out of town. It took weeks, preventing me from putting an obituary in the paper that would have information about a celebration of life. Before then, I had always had warm feelings about the University. The feelings were tied up with the time when Trip was there in school, the things he loved about it, and about himself when he was there as a student.

"Mom! I found out I can be anyone I want to be here", he said to me early in his first year.

 There were also memories and feelings from times I was there as a young girl: warm, fuzzy memories of the University town of Charlottesville. Back when I was in grade school, we went there from home in West Virginia to look for a pony for me. My father had some horse connections there from having gone to UVA one summer. I had memories of kind adults, the big farms on green rolling hills, of horses, their intoxicating aroma, of saddle leather, of the town being small and having cozy little diners that were fun for me even at that young age. There was Grover Van Devender, a sweet man, a horse dealer, and huntsman of the Farmington Hunt Club. He was a University of Virginia graduate. Those were times when Daddy was mellow and happy. He and Mother didn't fight. He was happy being in horse country and more or less on his good behavior. Mother didn't zap me with her words. I felt safe. None of the bad things happened there. I thought it was a place that would always be so. But my feelings started changing. I didn't like the University so much. It was disorienting to me from the perspective of a grieving parent. The safety and kindness were gone. I felt alone. And was trying to secure the chapel for a celebration of Trip's life.

 Soon, Dana and I went to Austin, through the house where Trip and Laura had been living. It was full of Trip's things. Laura was gone; moved out already. I wonder, did she blame me for Trip's suicide? Or could she possibly think that I blamed her? I was sure she was hurting, too. Perhaps seeing us would just be too much. I saw this moving out as a pattern for her. When life got too complex, or there was bad energy, she moved. She owned a real estate rental company, so it was familiar territory for her, but the pressure to hurry was difficult for me. She had canceled the rental and scheduled the utility cut-off. I think it was to happen in another day or two, at the most. I believed she meant well toward us, but she wanted to get away from the memories. I just couldn't hurry.

I looked around the home, a one-story brick house on a cement slab with a small, fenced backyard. I saw the garden hose still uncoiled and laying in the spot that must have been where Trip fell when he shot himself. The hose that washed away his blood. Trip's car was in the driveway in front of the garage door, the blue Hyundai Sonata that he was driving the last time I saw him alive. He had been pulling out of my driveway in July, two months before. I was hating to see him leave.

Why didn't I stop him?

I think I always hated to see the kids go, maybe like mothers everywhere when the kids leave. It was bittersweet because you wanted them to be fully engaged in their own lives, but you also wanted to keep them close. I have a photo Trip sent of himself on that same day. He stopped on his way out of Colorado to look at the Red Rocks Amphitheater in Denver. He was in shorts and his signature green t-shirt - this one said Costa Rica, and it was sleeveless, showing his well-developed arm muscles - along with the ever-present Teva sandals on his feet.

There was a lot of stuff in this house. All of it was Trip's.

"I don't like abandoning good things. I finally retired a t-shirt from 1981 not long ago. I need help throwing things away."

25 Random Things About Me #3". Trip Lucas, Facebook.

It hurt to see that house without Trip there. I saw his fingerprint everywhere. In the whimsical string of Christmas tree lights hanging across one wall year-round, in the pass-through from the kitchen that he had remodeled, and the work area with a desk for Laura that he built; in the bookshelves - he built them, too - with all his books. I thought it must have been the same shelving system that he built when he was in graduate school at the University of Texas here in Austin. I saw him in the massive bed that he had made with built-in drawers under it. He made that when he and Kim were married. It was like him to build something that was good-looking but also very useful. They needed the storage space. I see *him*. All this stuff. I need more time. Maybe not so much to sort through the things, but time to find the place in my heart where my love for Trip hangs out and where I need to find the room for his loss.

That's the thing: where do I put the loss? When I told my friend Craig, the co-owner of Vail Mountain Coffee and Tea, about Trip, he cried and immediately said,

"I don't know where to put that". Neither did I.

When Trip was young and still living at home, at our farm, he had a floor to ceiling bookshelf - full. A closet - full. Current things were in two piles on the floor. What always floors *me* is when I remember the time when he was somewhere away from home and wanted me to look for an address book and send him someone's address. He was able to tell me in which pile and where in the pile to find the right address book. I gave up trying to straighten his room and resorted to vacuuming around the piles. He says he retired a t-shirt. Really?

Laura was at work when Dana and I were there, and it felt as if she was avoiding us. Perhaps it was because she was feeling something toward us, but I didn't know what it was, if it was friendly or hostile. Could have been either.

Dana and I went through Trip's things, moving near and around each other, sometimes talking, some of the time lost in our own thoughts. I had lost my only son. Dana had lost her only brother. Strong, kick-ass Dana, my telemark-skiing, former smokejumper daughter, who became a nurse. She and Trip had recently been talking and supporting each other over their respective relationships that had been struggling. We were both going to miss him. It was not only painful, but eerie how different the space felt without him. When he was still here, stuff in his office was on the floor in piles. Now, someone had arranged a lot of it neatly on 6-foot-long tables. It looked ascetic, inanimate. There were boxes and boxes of saved letters from friends and family, digital books, print books, two large hard drives, two or three laptops, buckets of thumb drives and stored digital info, a huge collection of digital movies for which he is well-known among friends and family. There was an unquantifiable number of photos.

25 Random Things About Me #10, Trip Lucas, Facebook.

In Trip's closet full of hanging clothes, I was stopped by his tuxedo with red cummerbund. When he wasn't in a t-shirt, shorts, and Teva sandals, he looked most at home and happy in that tux. It was hard to decide what to do with it. What would I do with it if I kept it? Make a wax model and dress it in the tux? Not my style, but I don't know what to do. In the end, I didn't keep it. I have my memories and the photos of him wearing the tux. Laura had arranged for Goodwill to come pick up whatever we didn't want to keep, and the time was getting close. I hated to think about that – Goodwill taking stuff that I was trying to decide whether to keep or not.

I resented feeling rushed. This was more than I could handle in the allotted time and so soon, but like many things, what could I do about it? I can't undo anything that I have done in my life so far. I can't make any of it un-happen. I can't undo someone else's decisions or choices, either. Nor do I want to change most of it: certainly not being a mom or trying to grow away from the dictums of my parents and becoming – no matter how long it takes me - who I am. There are so many things over which we have no control. But people make U-turns every day, don't they? They realize they are going the wrong way and turn around. I say that to clients often when they think they can't change something in their lives. Yet, there are those times you can't turn around. The die is cast.

I took with me the two large photo albums that I made for Trip after he graduated from UVA and before the time Joe and I finally split. I knew the split was coming and made use of the time just before I started grad school to finally do something with each child's photos, report cards, art, camp photos - all of it. Each one has an album or two.

Everything from Trip's birth to the year I put the albums together, 1990, was in there: photos, report cards, art. I took some books. I thought I'd smell him in a shirt, so I took a couple of those - green ones. Turns out, I didn't smell anything. I took the letters and planned to give some to his friends who wrote them.

I saw Trip's toys - dart board, mountain bike, and climbing gear in the garage, along with yard and gardening equipment. The yard things reminded me of a time I was there and said to Trip about some of the plants in pots,

"Tell Laura that......"

"Mom, I am the one who takes care of the plants."

It's true. It took me until he was grown to realize how nurturing he was. He was pretty loud as a kid, squawking like a hen when he felt his sisters were stepping on his toes. He took up a lot of the energy. And provided a lot. I'm going to miss that nurturing side – along with all the rest of him. Just the year before that time, he had come out to Colorado to be with me after my hip replacement. He was between jobs – again - and had some time. He took care of the tomato plant that a friend gave me and wanting to "do" something, he put some insulation in where there wasn't any. He did that even though it seemed to invite the fear of an allergic reaction in him. He had always worried about his lungs, accusing my smoking in his early years for damaging them. They weren't damaged, as far as I know. I quit because I really wanted to and because the kids gave me a lot of grief about it – they would cough when I lit up, things like that. I am very happy they did that. My niece, Kee, even said one day when I lit up, "You're gonna die."

I knew I would miss his goofy, silly ways, too. His giant-sized enthusiasm. His humor. The wide-ranging curiosity. How widely he read. And so much else. How can this be real? I was so frustrated I wanted to cry but didn't or couldn't. How could this ever be all right? I understood that I might get used to life without Trip, but it would never be all right. And now, time itself seems unreliable, not one of those things I can take for granted - a tomorrow, a sunrise, a hope for something in the future, an expectation like health or happiness.

Chapter Four

"Drugs: Despite my name, except for puffs I can count on one hand and two brownies from friends, I've never had the desire to even try any drugs. I've avoided aspirin most of my life. However, I used to eat 20 Krispy Kremes in one sitting (they used to make a 20 box). That may count as drugs because I usually enjoyed the lovely, knackered sleep afterwards. Including skydiving, rock climbing, windsurfing, skiing, etc., I've also inadvertently enjoyed a little adrenaline."

25 Random Things About Me #12, Trip Lucas, Facebook.

I left Austin and flew back to Colorado. Again. The first time was after the trip to Virginia to confer with the rest of the family. Pulling into my garage, I noticed Trip's brand-new mountain bike. He had one at his home in Austin, so this one he had bought the year before to leave here. Seeing it was another reminder. I still couldn't quite take it in. I wouldn't ever again see Trip on that bike. Or hear him talking to me, telling me, "Mom, you can't hang this up on the wall because of the disk brakes." Really? is what I thought when he told me. But at the time, it was his new baby, and he was protective of it and certain that it should not hang. I meant to investigate that because I could swear I had seen them hanging in bike shops. But I didn't investigate. A few years later, I bought myself a road bike that had disk brakes, and I got my question answered. They *can* hang. I was told to pump the brakes a bit before riding to make sure any air was out of the line. This bike joined the growing collection of Trip's toys at my house – tumpline, climbing gear, lots of climbing gear, ski clothes for him and Laura, and bits I can't identify. A part of me was still thinking that this whole situation was not permanent, as if Trip was coming back. As if he was just down in Austin or somewhere that's not here, but still in life. Another part was planning a celebration of his life. Two of them. One for Virginia and one for Texas.

———

Years ago, while riding my horse, I heard a cow bellowing, keening like I'd never heard before. As I got closer, I saw an enormous oak tree sheltering the cow who was standing over her dead young calf. She had her head raised up to the heavens, crying her heart out, feet splayed as if they could barely keep her standing in her grief. It broke my heart. I wanted to go to her and comfort her. Now I am that cow.

I was a mother bear when the kids were growing up. Once, for example, the kids and I went to the auto dealership for the third time for the same problem, which was still not fixed. The head mechanic had told me to come at 8:30 in the morning, that there would be no charge and it would take 30 minutes. Of course, it took much longer. The kids got restless and fussy during the first hour. Trip kept wanting to open the showroom cars' doors or to climb up on the outside of the cars. I kept holding him back. When an hour stretched into the second hour, I told Trip he could have at it. When all five got even fussier and lunchtime was approaching, I politely asked if there were a loaner car that I could use to take them to lunch. The insensitive answer was, "Can't you just walk somewhere?"

I said, "Not with five under five; no, I cannot just walk somewhere out on 4 Lane Broad St."

Broad St. is US 250 and a main thoroughfare with two or three lanes of traffic in each direction. After three-plus hours and restless, fussy kids who were now very hungry, the car was ready. I got in line to pick up the keys. Just as the woman told me there was a bill to pay, someone who must have been a strong and unthinking adult let three-year-old Antoinette through the heavy glass door at Richmond Ford onto the huge car lot. In an instant, I was both furious and panicky. I don't remember what I did about my other four kids with me, but I charged back to the head mechanic, saying in a rather strong tone of voice that my daughter had been let loose outside where there were hundreds of cars, some of them moving. The man turned pale, got on his loudspeaker, and announced that all hands should stop what they were doing and go out to look for this child. Fortunately for everyone, she was found by one of the mechanics just before a car was about to back over her.

When I told her about it, Mother said to me, "Oh, you're just like your father." That was her way of belittling me for getting people's attention, for making a fuss, being demanding, just like Daddy. Yet, to me, I was defending my young. What's so wrong about that? My child could have been killed in that parking lot.

Mother's shaming was just one of the many times that one parent or the other squashed me, the real me, and left *me* more and more lost in a dark, hidden place.

Saying I was just like my father was a put-down, whereas my father would say, "You're just like your mother." The last time I remember he said it was when their friend, Ann, died. She and her husband were life-long friends of my parents. I was visiting my parents at the time, standing in the kitchen talking with my father when he told me. Spontaneously, I reached for Mother's address book that was right there on the counter, saying that I wanted to send Ann's husband a note of condolence. My father shouted at me, "You're just like your mother," as if it was a bad thing I wanted to do or that I was too "much." That's often how I felt around Daddy, as if I was just too much of anything, not subdued and contained enough. Too full of life, and he wanted to poke a hole in me to drain it out of me. There were so many things I never said to my parents because of the reaction I knew I would get. It was like both parents to not want to hear any complaints, questions, or opinions from me, regardless of why. They encouraged me to be silent, to have no voice. *They* were the voice of the patriarchal culture that had prevailed for centuries.

Fast forward almost 30 years. I was in my own home after the divorce. The one with the loan that Trip had co-signed instead of my father. Mother and Daddy had been there overnight – first and only time ever – and were pulling out of the driveway. As they backed up, my father leaned out the window and said in his most gruff and loud, authoritative voice, the one that always scared me and made me cower, "Next time I come, I want to see that garage fixed!" Both painted metal overhead doors of the detached garage looked beaten up. The one on the left didn't open or close and it was seriously bent out of shape in places. The other one worked – by hand when I got out of the car to push it up - but it didn't look so hot, either. It was also bent up a fair amount and starting to rust. The garage also needed a new roof and a paint job. At Daddy's comment, some indignant part of me erupted.

"You'd better not come back for a long time because I can't afford it right now," I shouted back at him.

 Neither of us said another word, but wow, did that feel good. They never did come back. Daddy had no idea that I was earning enough to pay my mortgage, office rent, and other bills. Just not enough to include a few thousand-dollar fix-up of the garage. I don't think he even knew what my profession was or what I did for a living. And, if you can hear me now, Daddy, a public school teacher's salary, then would not have been enough for all my living expenses.

Within a year or so, I was visiting one of my sisters in West Virginia and went by to see my parents. While I was there, Daddy said that he and Mother wanted to talk with me about something. Just those words started up a dread in my gut and a buzzing in my head, but I followed them into the room where Daddy had his desk. The big, old, heavy yellow oak office desk that his father had used before my father took over the business. It looked industrial and out of place in this room. I assume my father was attached to it and the memory/prestige of being the president of the company. They sat down, mother on a chair beside the desk. I sat on a wooden loveseat across the room, the only other seat. Daddy swiveled around in his desk chair to look at me when he spoke. The first words out of his mouth were, in his solemn-lecture tone of voice, "Now, we don't want to have to happen what happened last time." I had no idea what he meant; what last time? I didn't ask because, in seconds, I was petrified, dissociating (not out of my body up on the ceiling as often described by sexual assault victims, but I was somewhere out of my body and gasping for breath). I did not hear another word until my father began saying something like "let us know," signaling that this lecture had ended. Nodding my head, I said that I would as I got up to leave, still stiff with fear and still in the dark as to what I was agreeing to do. That same kind of thing happened to me more than once when I was a kid. This time, I was far from childhood.

Months later, I got a call from my parents saying that I hadn't let them know about the garage. From what they said, I gathered that they – my father – had offered to pay for garage repairs. I began to look for a contractor who might do the work and went so far as to discuss what I found out with my father. I regret agreeing to let him finance that project. As it proceeded, he barked at me more than once about this or that detail, including how I wanted him to pay – write a check to the contractor or to me. I didn't know and why did it matter? Which did he prefer? I wondered but did not ask and was, again, afraid of my father and only wanted to end the episode, to be far away from that moment in time and my sense of belittlement. Afterward, my sister Antoinette told me that Daddy was annoyed that I didn't send him a photo. Of course, he was annoyed and disappointed. I never got otherwise from him. I didn't think of it because my fear of him and his temper overrode my manners. The last thing in his life he said to me was, "I'm so disappointed in you," with a stern, glaring look, eyes almost red. One of my biggest regrets is that I didn't have the inner strength – enough faith in myself – to say to him what I felt in my heart, what his harsh manner did to me, "You are disappointed in *me*? Did you ever think that I might be disappointed in you? I have always been afraid of you, your temper, your sexual innuendos, and your abuse of everyone in this family. It all disappoints me."

———

I have a need to allow Trip, or anyone, compassion for the pain and confusion that surrounds such a decision. In July, when he told me that he and Laura were fighting and that she wasn't *The One,* I wish now that I had asked him to tell me about the fights, what they were about, and why she wasn't the one. On his last day, the last time we talked, I wish I had asked him to tell me about his pain and what he felt when he thought about having to live through a breakup. I could have asked what the hardest thing about it was. But I was afraid, gripped by fear. If he still insisted that he didn't think he could live through the break-up, I might have asked him what he would miss most about being alive or not being around to enjoy. The truth is, I didn't think of those questions at the time. I was paralyzed by fear. I could barely breathe.

Then, there's always 'do you have a plan for taking your life.' As a therapist, I knew or had been taught most of those things, but I let my fear take over. Fear is a monster. It is paralyzing. I have lived way too much of my life in fear – most often of my parents, of never living according to their calcified ways, but maybe I have been equally afraid of my own strength. Is that possible? For a very long time, I didn't know it was there. Then, getting pregnant and unwed……well, that sealed it once and for all. I didn't know that years later, I would be able to tell myself, as my therapist did, "At least you followed your instincts." A way of self-compassion and understanding. But in this case, with Trip's suicide, the fear had its way.

Trip always had trouble with a breakup. He said his big fear was abandonment. He *wrote* that it was. And this time, he told me that he didn't think he could live through another breakup. I had no response. I had lost my voice, my words, how Daddy wanted me to be. Mother, too, for that matter. Don't be too much. Don't want too much. Don't stand out. Don't believe in yourself. Heck, they were saying, you don't have a self – we own you.

Trip not only had my full-time attention before Antoinette and Kate were born, but he had me all to himself back then. His dad, Joe, was out of town five days a week for work. I wish now that I had prepared Trip by talking more about becoming a big brother and having a baby brother or sister. I know he would have understood some of it. He was good with Antoinette and Kate but showed the strain when his grandmother or some other person would come over and talk just to me and not to Trip. One evening, when Joe was out of town, his mother and brother John came over to help feed Antoinette and Kate. When his grandmother kept talking to me, Trip showed he was feeling neglected by taking 33 albums out of the cabinet and stepping on them. It didn't hurt them, but he let me know he didn't like not having *some*one's attention. Especially mine.

I will always remember the moment when Trip was four, and he said to me one day:

"I wish we had a boy my age living in our same house."

At the time I thought he was prescient because within a very short time - weeks - a family moved in across the street. They had a son named Tripp, who was just 12 days older than Trip. They were still friends and both living in Texas, different cities, when Trip took his life.

When Trip told me that July day that he and Laura were fighting, he had not had a job for months, not since his last software contract. Laura was after him to get a job, any old job. I suspect he felt ineffective and emasculated by that. I think that time in his life was like when his marriage with Kim was stressful. Trip's dot.com job had ended, and he was without a good job for a long time. That's when he took so many part-time jobs, most of which he liked, but it didn't make him happy to be unable to find the job for which he was educated. Then he got bronchitis, his body expressing what he might not have been able to do.

Writing has helped me to see how Trip and I shared some traits. We both felt things very deeply. I know he absorbed a lot of how I felt, too. A high school friend of Trip's said about him that he was so intuitive and that he must have felt things very deeply. He did. He felt he couldn't live through those times when his feelings and caring weren't reciprocated. He would rather die than not have love. I wonder, was it harder for him because he had experienced love from me, at least, and his great grandparents? And probably some others? When I was young, I thought a little about dying, but I think I was much more stoic than Trip. I put up with so much denigration and lack of love that I didn't love myself. I thought I just had to keep doing my best to please others, and that's how I would get anything in return - if I ever did. I hope Trip loved himself.

As I plan, I think Trip would like the University of Virginia chapel as the venue for a celebration of his life. It is where he started to come into his own. He loved the learning, the people, and being able to use his athletic ability by joining the wrestling team as a walk-on. The meals, especially breakfast, made him happy. He loved cereal, usually sweet and lots of it, for breakfast or snacks, so the University dining hall, with its huge dispensers full of cereal, some of it sugary, was sheer delight to him. It was one of the first things he showed me.

Since Kate lived in Charlottesville, Virginia, where the University is located, she had been helpful in discussing the logistics of that location. As for a date for the chapel, she said, "Don't pick a football weekend. Parking would be impossible." I thought that my other daughters were more or less ok with the place whenever we could get it. Since Joe had washed his hands of the whole idea, that was one less person to consult.

One day, irritated with the ongoing run-around from the University, I asked, "Is there an assistant I might speak with?" Then I mentioned the names of a couple of friends who were influential at the University. In nanoseconds, I suppose thanks to the dropped names, the assistant answered the phone. In another week or two, I had a date that, because of the wait, would be almost two months after Trip's death. He died on September 10th. The memorial will be on November 8th.

I was feeling what I imagined it must be like to walk on the moon – completely ungrounded, with no gravity to keep me down, no familiar guidelines. My daughters all lived somewhere else and were busy working and going on with their lives, so I didn't discuss much of this with them except for Kate's logistical advice. It added to my feeling of being untethered, blowing in the wind.

 Finally, I could put together an obituary. I put it in the Richmond Times Dispatch (Virginia) with the details of the memorial celebration included. Considering the way people had become scattered these days, there was no one way to reach everyone who would want to know but using Facebook in addition to the newspaper helped. Still, some people fell through the cracks and don't get any word at all – my college roommate, for one. She was the one who introduced Joe and me and had a somewhat proprietary interest. She and her husband didn't live in Richmond, but I failed to think of that.

Now what? I asked myself. We had a date. Where should I start on that event that I never dreamed would happen in the first place? Kate had recently been to the life celebration for a cousin of Joe's. She had been working with him in a well-known advertising business. He was beloved and died too soon. She had some suggestions based on how his memorial was organized. Because of that I started thinking about a slide show from Trip's life. That was a bit scary because of Mother's many belittling comments about me. I could be struck with little confidence in my ability when faced with something new, creative, or important to me. How, then, was I going to do this thing that meant so much to me?

I was in the middle of a storm and trying to survive. I saw people at the grocery store or the post office and I was unable to recall names in some cases. It had been eight years since I moved here to Colorado, and I'd never looked back, but at this moment, I felt disoriented. Some of what I did was give in to the magical belief that if I thought hard enough or daydreamed hard enough, I could change what happened and make it go away. I was not sleeping at all well. I got in bed each night, and even if my mind wasn't going in circles, my body did not seem to settle down, as if it was not tired or was afraid to relax for fear of not ever coming out of it, of just drifting off in some not quite present state of being. If I did sleep, I woke up several times a night feeling terrible dread and disbelief. I tried Ambien, but then I felt too drugged, so I put that aside. I was physically exhausted.

I'd never created a slide show before. I pulled out boxes and boxes of photos, searched through them, remembered, laughed, cried, selected, and scanned or not. There was a youthful me holding infant Trip when he was just home from the hospital. My body remembered – and could feel – all the times I held Trip and how he clung to me like a monkey. He was easy to carry because of that – no sack of potatoes. There was a one-year-old Trip on my parents' screened porch. He was holding a red, white, and blue ball with an impish smile on his face as if he knew something we didn't know. There was a teen-age Trip in Canada on vacation, arms crossed, sitting very still in a rustic Adirondack chair. He was looking down at a dish of ice cream on the chair's arm. There was a small red squirrel with its head, both front legs, and one back leg reaching into the bowl. There were countless ones of Trip climbing up big rock faces. And one of him with his arm around his wife, Kim, squatting down in a field of Texas Bluebonnets. There was another Trip with Laura in Texas in a field of yellow flowers. Going through Trip's lifetime in photos was sad and too much of a reminder of why I was doing it. But having the commitment to the project got me up each day and I was driven to make it happen. For me, if no one else. I was thinking that so many of my friends, and even some of Trip's, knew him in snippets of his life. I wanted this to be an overview. I didn't realize at the outset that this would also give me a creative fix. Learning how to do it, choosing music to go with it and how to make it all go together is satisfying and heartbreaking at the same time.

I was touched by the Apple tech man who stayed on the phone with me for two whole hours as he taught me how to sync music with the slides. He did not make me feel ignorant or rush me; he just stayed with me. It was as if the Apple man was taking me by the hand and showing me where each little command was on the movie app, which came on my laptop. I was amazed and a bit chagrinned when he pointed out the steps that were there for the taking to apply the music. You just have to be patient enough to read the fine print. I had chosen, with a little help from a knowledgeable country music friend, two-step music. It spoke to that part of Trip that loved to dance. He spent time teaching the two-step to some of the young women when he was stationed in Georgia for part of his army obligation. I have photos of him doing just that. Now, George Strait's "I Just Want to Dance with You" brings tears to my eyes whenever I hear it, along with "It Just Comes Natural." I wish Trip were with me, too, helping me with his unconventional, creative, and serious/humorous approach.

Days blended together. I went from the photos and scanning them to Trip's piles of letters: from me, his sisters, other family, and his many friends. It appeared that he never threw any of them away. One of those was from a schoolgirl, now grown, Virginia, who was a student at St. Catherine's School when Trip was one of the leaders of the outdoor program. She wanted to go skydiving. She had some money saved up, but her parents said "no." She begged Trip, the leader and older man (just out of undergrad), to go with her on the sly, seeing him as someone wiser and safe but also daring.

He agreed – with some trepidation – and one day, they drove to the Hartwood Paracenter in Hartwood, Virginia, about 40 miles north of Richmond. Each of them received an Accelerated Freefall Certificate to commemorate the event. It was a never-forgotten moment for both – her parents, too, I later discovered when I met her father at a party. He said to me,

"Oh, you're the Lucas whose son took my daughter skydiving"! He seemed quite ok with it by then.

Many of Trip's friends are dear to me, and reading their words on Facebook, I felt both warm and sad as they spoke of many of his endearing traits and funny episodes. Add the letters to the outpouring from them at his death. His friend from UVA, Christine Van Dusen Butler, wrote, "He was the face of pure love."

I kept Joe apprised of what I was doing and of any expenses I incurred. He didn't respond, which I assumed was because he didn't want a memorial in the first place. Or he was afraid of being hit up to contribute to costs. Either was possible, but I didn't ask, and years later still don't know the answer.

I had clients, though I had cut back before then to think about my future. In one way, seeing them was as therapeutic for me as it was for them. I questioned whether to cancel all appointments, but things seemed to work themselves out. There was one person who had been coming to me for licensure supervision since she was going to become a counselor herself. When I asked her to take a few weeks off, and I told her why, she apparently didn't process what I had said and, one day, insisted on coming over *now* because she was very close to reaching the hours she needed to finish. She wanted to be able to apply for her license and get her practice started. I understood that, but I was in no frame of mind or heart to be able to give her anything helpful. Still, she pushed me to hurry things along and soon – without an appointment – brought over the papers she needed to have signed, still not understanding. I felt invisible. Did she not hear me? Or understand me? When I told her again about my loss, I lost it when she said,

"I know what you are going through."

I was as shocked by her apparent inability to hear what I had told her as I was by her insensitive response. Clearly, I had not finished my job with her. She had stopped her car on the street, just beyond the entrance to my driveway, and reached through her window to hand me the papers. Then, she got out of her car, and we were standing at the edge of my driveway.

"You do *not* know. You have no idea whatsoever", I tell her, my voice raised in fury, my fists clenched. She reached out to pet my puppy, asking at the same time if it was okay.

"Leave her alone," I said. I was a junkyard dog, cornered and baring my teeth. Angry was how I felt then and felt as I wrote about that moment. I was thinking, "How dare she? How can she possibly be so insensitive?"

In addition to my heightened emotional state, I found I had to attend to the legal side of that journey. That meant dealing with Trip's financial and business life. It was almost more than I could comprehend, let alone handle. Included was his grad school loan that he had been still paying off. There was his 401K – I discovered that I was the beneficiary. I was touched and cried over that. There was his auto and renter's insurance with USAA. USAA does not make this easy due to all the t's it wants to be crossed and the i's that need to be dotted. It takes nothing for granted and wants absolute proof of everything, the car's ownership, for example. I pulled my hair out, trying to unearth the car's title, to no avail. I was trying to cancel the auto insurance but couldn't do that if the car would be driven. To make it all harder, there was a long-winded employee who was the agent I had to deal with. He kept mentioning how great Trip's service was. I am pretty sure the man was a veteran himself. If he had only known how much Trip did not like the military. I wouldn't dare tell him for fear of what his reaction might be. He might decide I am not worth helping at all.

I couldn't give the car to Laura, who said at first that she would like to have it, because I couldn't give it away without the title. I made frustrating call after frustrating call to Texas state offices and courts, hoping to be issued another title for the car because no one seemed to know where Trip's copy was. Laura got fed up with my constant calls and questions. She blasted me, much as I did my client, and said she wanted nothing to do with "the damn car" or *me*. In the end, the title was in the glove compartment, discovered by Trip's friend, Jean-Philippe. Jean-Philippe had agreed, after Laura's outburst, to keep the car at his place. Later, he bought the car from Trip's estate.

It was as if there was a huge hole in my heart that was keeping the blood from pumping through my body and causing it to drain out instead so that I felt devoid of my life's blood. With each breath, more life force drained out of me. Death certificates: everyone wanted one or a copy of one. The funeral home told me that I would need at least ten of them. The very words *death certificate* raised the hair on the back of my neck and caused me to sink deeply into myself. Deep breaths – I kept taking them as I wrote, hoping it would soothe me.

As a therapist, I had witnessed how the death of a child often caused a couple to split, but Joe and I were already split. For us, the divide remained the same. We didn't talk to each other at all. I had long ago learned that I could not count on him to be present for me in most ways. He was oblivious to how I felt. He often told me that I wasn't feeling what I was feeling or that I didn't have anything to worry about regarding whatever it was that concerned me. Period, end of discussion for him. When my obstetrician discovered a lump in one breast, he sent me to a surgeon who tried to aspirate it and couldn't. He told me that he was pretty sure this wasn't a cancerous thing but wouldn't know until he removed it. The night before I was due to have the surgery, I told Joe that I was scared, that I didn't want cancer, and that I wanted to live long enough to see our kids grow up. He said, irritated, "You don't have cancer." I didn't, but what hurt was his not being able to empathize with my fear of the possibility. That, and having to take a cab to the hospital for the surgery. Joe went to work as usual that morning. I wanted to leave the car for Sally, who would be there with the kids, just in case one of them had some emergency and she needed the car. Our youngest two had just turned three years old at the time.

————

Nineteen years before the time of Trip's loss, I was still getting myself together after the divorce, living in a rented house a few miles from the farm where the kids grew up. I had opened my private psychotherapy practice a year before, which was paying for itself, but I had just enough to buy food and pay my house and office rent. The owners of the house wanted to sell it, and I wanted to buy it. My banker brother-in-law told me that I could qualify for an FHA loan as a first-time homebuyer. The FHA agent told me that "to qualify for an FHA loan, you need to have two years' worth of income from a previous job or have a co-buyer." I didn't have the two years – only 18 months. In that amount of work at a mental health agency, I had the required work hours and hours of supervision to get my state license and hang out my shingle. Earlier than some. I thought that was a good thing, but it turned out not so good for the FHA. Hoping against hope, knowing him, for a little mercy or kindness from my father, I asked him if he would be my co-buyer, hoping he might since it would cost him no money. It wasn't my best shot because he was stingy and believed in not helping us kids with anything. He said to me when he walked me down the aisle at my wedding,

"You're on your own now."

He briefly considered being my co-borrower but began to get offended as I told him of the personal and financial information the lenders wanted from him. It felt intrusive to this man who prided himself on his reputation as a good businessman, respected in his community. He prided himself on being well-regarded by the president of his bank. He was full of pride, maybe even pompous at times. One night, he and Mother called to lecture me, though Daddy did all the talking, saying in booze-slurred speech,

"Your Mother and I have decided" … that they wouldn't help me. That he wouldn't co-sign my loan. That

"You should have kept your teaching certificate" – from 30 years before.

Apparently, he did not understand – or didn't want to – that I had a viable way of supporting myself, that I was self-employed, but that I needed a co-borrower because of lender requirements. Not because I needed money from him. Part of me was relieved. The thought of enduring a protracted relationship with him centered on borrowing money, even if not from him, was frightening. I shocked myself by hanging up the phone in mid-lecture. For years, I had kept going, no matter how my parents treated me, and I had let go of any expectations. Yet, if I had any doubts about distancing myself from them, here was proof of why I had done it. And now, I realize how infantilizing it would have been to have had my father as co-borrower. He would have felt entitled to ask me all kinds of nosy questions about how I managed my finances and more. Later, he did exactly that in the garage episode.

At the time, I was disappointed. I had thought that being a homebuyer would be a start at establishing credit in my own name – something that at the ripe age of 54 would be a good thing. I had no health insurance except a $5000 deductible catastrophe policy. The Cobra from marriage, and later from my counseling agency job, had run out – and I had no savings. Joe, an investment banker, had gambled in the market with his/our considerable earnings and lost. As far as I knew, he had drained our 401K to cover his investment losses. In addition, he had never invested in an IRA for either of us.

There was a part of me that was starting to feel a sense of freedom and strength I had never known. I *knew* in the deepest fibers of my being that I was going to be all right. Eventually, this was a setback. I was trying to swallow it. That's when Trip came to visit. I thought a long time before he arrived about whether to tell him my attempted home purchase story. When he arrived, I still wasn't sure, but then I told him. For what seemed like a long time, he was silent, and I wondered if he was thinking that I was crazy to think about buying a house with next to no money or that I was crazy to ask my harsh, tight-wad father for help. Finally, he said,

"I will be your co-borrower, mom. You should have a nice place to live".

I was moved to tears and filled with love and gratitude. What a beautiful thing for him to suggest. What generosity of spirit, let alone something as tangible as his limited financial worth. It took me several minutes to fully fathom his offer. Trip was young, not long out of graduate school, and just starting out. At the time, he had the best income he had ever had in his life and was feeling expansive and helpful.

"Trip, that is so generous of you. Wow. Can you really handle it? Financially, I mean? And if I were to accept, I would want to get you off the loan as soon as I possibly can."

"I can handle it, Mom."

Overwhelmed, I caught my breath, had an internal debate, and asked him about his cost-of-living expenses plans for the next couple of years. Then, I accepted his offer, and he became my co-buyer for what turned out to be the next four years. After that, I was able to re-finance and get Trip off the loan. I had hoped to do it in two years but wasn't able.

———

Now, I was at this moment that was several weeks since Trip's death, and I finally had a date for the memorial. I needed to find a place after the service where people could gather and where there could also be food service. I made calls to caterers and event spaces in Charlottesville and within the University to compare menus and prices and/or rental costs. I felt gouged or stumped everywhere I turned. Or the space was too big or unavailable. There were quite a few restaurants that catered and plenty of caterers but comparing them wasn't apples to apples. Some offered this food or that service, but not together. Some had a space I could rent or that they provided with the food, but others didn't. Some had one kind of food but not another. When I kept hitting dead ends on that front, I tried another one. It was taxing and required a clear and detached mind, neither of which I had. I didn't live nearby anymore – about 2500 miles away – another difficulty. Looking back, I was grateful that even though I often felt so alone, having lost Trip and being the only one making plans for his memorials, I also had years of being able to rely on myself under my belt. Not all of those were after marriage. Quite a few were during marriage.

After a plethora of calls and conversations later, a friend of Kate's offered to sponsor us at The Colonnade Club. It had an available event space just the right size and was perfectly located on university grounds. Whew. That began a whole new round of caterers to call, all of whom were from a list provided by the Colonnade Club, all of them expensive, at least for my budget. The University and the town had turned into a resort of sorts – highly sought after and highly-priced with limited availability of most commodities.

Finally, I picked a caterer, one with a good menu with several vegan options (my preferred diet), and that was used for the venue. I arranged for those of us family who would be in town to have dinner at the caterer's restaurant the evening before the celebration. That was a happy decision, and it felt good to have us together. Joe and his brothers weren't there since they would be driving in on the day of the service. My sisters and those of their kids and spouses who could come were there the night before.

With the catering and space arranged, I was free to turn to the celebration itself. As I did, I spoke with the woman who was assigned to me as the contact between me and the chapel. At first, she was kind and solicitous, no doubt sucking up to me because she'd been told that I had connections. Things changed when I told her that, no, I did not need to have the large free-standing cross placed front and center. After that, she was clearly disapproving. It's probably good that she hadn't read one of Trip's collection of quotes:

"God is an ever-receding packet of scientific ignorance."

~ Neil DeGrasse Tyson

Or the Random Thing, in which he mentioned that he was an atheist who studied Buddhism.

She also curtly let me know that it was necessary to use the tech people hired by the University. I had concerns because my slideshow was on an Apple laptop. I wanted the techs there in time to make what adjustments might be needed to access my Apple vs a PC. She assured me, in her newly crusty attitude toward me, that they could take care of it. I was skeptical.

Kate's suggestions included having people who were willing to say a few words about Trip at the celebration. I came up with some people to ask if they would like to speak: people who were important to Trip or those to whom Trip was important. I called Townley first. He was also the first non-family member I called after Trip's death. He was Trip's ninth-grade science teacher and leader of the outdoor program. He took Trip on his first rock climbs. Climbing became Trip's life-long passion, though he had many interests. Townley was a great support to Trip as both his teacher and, later, Trip and Townley became good friends. He is someone for whom I have high regard and much warmth for how he mentored Trip and for what he meant to Trip.

Kate asked a couple of Trip's friends whom she thought would like to contribute. Seeing Trip's Facebook page go viral with condolences and memories was almost too much because it forced me out of my denial of his death. I had accepted that his loss was real when, on some level, I was still refusing to do that. I didn't want it to be true.

Focus and planning didn't come easily at that time, but ideas and thoughts kaleidoscope around in my mind. I caught a few of them. One of those was a program to hand out at the memorial. I liked the one a childhood friend had had for his wife's service. It was simple and personal on unassuming paper. Using that as my inspiration, I began to create one for Trip's memorial. It was on cream-colored card stock about 4 x 6 inches when folded in half from top to bottom. On the front, there was a photo of a red rock stupa near Redstein Crag in Redstone, Colorado. It is where Trip last rock-climbed in

Colorado in July with his friend Jeff. There were Tibetan prayer flags blowing in the wind above the stupa. Across the bottom of the photo, I have printed the words from Kahlil Gibran:

"When you are sorrowful, look again in your heart, and you shall see that, in truth, you are weeping for that which has been your delight."

The stupa was where I took some of Trip's ashes in the Spring following his death. Jeff Jackson and his wife Hannah guided me up there and shared with me the sight of Trip's ashes blowing out with the wind. Blowing beyond the prayer flags.

Chapter Five

"Overtly religious people scare me. I grew up Catholic and switched to Episcopalian at 14. I now call myself Episcopalian to humor scary people, but I am an atheist who studies Buddhism. I like the quote by Oscar Wilde when someone asked him if he believed in God. He responded by saying "No, I believe in something much bigger."

25 Random Things About me #19. Trip Lucas, Facebook.

On the day of the first celebration of Trip's life, so many pieces went haywire. Especially me. I left the programs in the back of Kate's car that went back to her house with her when she jogged the few miles over to pick it up. I had driven it over to the chapel since I needed to be there when it opened – which didn't happen at the stated time. It was becoming apparent that the chapel folks were a bit loose with time and schedules. The crusty lady told me to call her if it wasn't open when I arrived. It wasn't. And then I left the programs in the car. I recovered from that one, but there are others.

I was nervous enough that I seemed to have lost all my social skills, such as greeting people when they walked toward the pews. And toward me since I was standing up front. And maybe saying "thank you for coming" because I was grateful for each and everyone who did. I might have been standing on my hands if I didn't have on a skirt, just because it would be easier, something I already knew how to do, than what was about to happen.

I was angry that the tech people the University provided were almost an hour late, the hour during which I had made at least two calls to the university lady, the crusty one. Each time I called, she said, "They're on the way." They were supposed to hook up to my laptop for the slide show and have it working at least a half hour before the time the service was scheduled. But they were not there fifteen minutes before. I had planned to have the slide show play for 30 minutes (two run-throughs) beforehand while people were walking in and being seated. I was unable to even try to recover the fumble at that point now that it was five or ten minutes to start time. I had been sitting in the front pew with my MacBook Pro on my lap for a long time before the tech people arrived. They were coming and going from a side room where the tech controls are located. I was appalled and almost frozen inside, unable to improvise or to move. It seemed there was nothing to do but go on. Two or three minutes before it was scheduled to begin, Townley came over to ask me if I wanted to wait for the slide show. I said that I would like to give them another minute or two.

Finally, just as Townley started walking toward the lectern and we were going ahead with the memorial, the tech guys managed to connect to the slide show on my MacBook. We let it run through once, and then Townley began.

I was, and am, touched by what Trip's friends had to say about him and by their poise and graciousness. I loved hearing of their experiences of Trip and was grateful to them for giving their time to be present. And to Townley, of course, as both his teacher and his friend. The man whom Trip called periodically with the greeting, "Hey Bop!"

I never even thought about speaking. I was barely able to hold myself together, let alone get up and speak. I never asked Joe if he was interested. I didn't think of asking him, probably because he didn't want to have any celebration in the first place. I wasn't even sure he'd be there, though I did think he wouldn't want to appear indifferent by not coming. He was there, but he didn't bring Anne, which made me realize that she and Joe probably thought I meant not to come to this event since I had asked that she not be there for the first meeting with Joe and the girls. I did not mean to exclude her permanently. I regret not making that clear. I told her that next time I saw her.

Time stretched out. Both Carter and Dana had gone over their suggested time limit, and I perceived a restlessness in the chapel. Relief came when Dana was speaking, saying loving things about her brother, how she had on her cowboy boots for dancing, because Trip loved to dance, and at that very moment, the chapel bell rang the hour. A ripple of laughter went through those assembled. I think some imagined that Trip had rung the bell. With family, friends, and Trip's friends there, I felt for the first time in two months, for that moment, that I had stepped outside of an isolation booth. I felt surrounded by the warmth of friends. I still carry my parental wound that finds it hard to believe in or absorb warmth and love because my introjected belief is that I'm not worthy of it.

It mattered so much to me to do this memorial. There was, and is, an ache in my being that may never go away, but it seems that a memorial shares his memory and blesses it in a way. It blesses me, too, by having others present.

When Joe told me after the memorial, "You were a good Mother to Trip," I started thinking, who am I without him here in life? I am his mother, and of course, I am a mother to our four daughters. That's part of my identity. I am still working on the rest of it – the one after having raised the kids – or in addition to being a parent and a therapist – that maybe I should have discovered sooner. Losing Trip leaves a hole in my *identity* along with the one in my heart. Who am I now? I'm not sure. Until now, I didn't know the depth of what I said so many times another parent lost a child, "It's a parent's worst nightmare." No matter what, I will always love Trip and be the mom who loved him from before he was born. I thought his birth was the most beautiful thing that had ever happened to me from that day forward – really, from knowing I was pregnant with him. It had turned out to be a natural birth, which also made it memorable. And it was my first.

It isn't that the others weren't just as awesome, but they were different and not my first.

We walked from the chapel on the red brick walkway that is part of the hallowed, Thomas-Jefferson-designed grounds of The Lawn to go to The Colonnade Club to gather. The Lawn is part of the original academic village that Jefferson envisioned. It is where the first-built student and faculty housing spaces connect on facing sides to form two edges of The Lawn, a rectangle. On one of the short ends is the Jefferson-designed Rotunda. Inspired by the Pantheon in Rome, it was designed to represent the "authority of nature and the power of reason."

Trip's graduation was held there on that very lawn. On the day of his life celebration, it felt as if his graduation was a million years ago. The brick-paved path we were walking on seemed to exude history, including some of mine, as we strolled along. A shiver passed through me. Going inside, I wound up standing near the door and became an unintended receiving line while still trying to do what people seem to do these days: put up photos of the departed. I think one of my daughters must have remembered to bring photos. I don't remember doing it.

 For the rest of the afternoon, I was at one end of the large space, watching small groups of friends gather and talk, including Joe, talking and laughing with friends. I was too exhausted and sad to circulate. Finally, I sat down. I felt as if I must look like a much older woman, one wearing nylon stockings with the tops rolled down to just above the knees, with the rolls showing and white skin exposed above them. I was not wearing stockings at all, but my feet and legs were tired from high-heeled fashion boots. What a bad idea that was. I wore a green sweater since it was Trip's first color choice. A few of my friends, along with my sisters, found me there and had a brief sit with me. My friend Sydna wanted to make sure I had eaten and brought me a plate.

I thought about how much Trip would have felt at home in this crowd and would have made it his. He had grown and learned but in essence, had changed little from the guy who spent his undergrad years here. He still loved his friends – and mine – and would enjoy each one. I watched his sisters enjoy their Lucas cousins, along with one of their cousins from my family, Betsy's son. They all seemed to be happy to see each other.

———

I thought about the slide show again and a few images of Trip at the farm where our kids spent most of their growing years. When Trip was nine, we bought part of a former – no cows by then – dairy farm about 20 miles west of the city of Richmond, Virginia. It was just a mile or two north of the James River. It suited us. Trip was very at home there. He enjoyed many aspects, among them the fence building, the animals, and some of the gardening – not so much when I asked the kids to help pull weeds in the truck-farm-sized vegetable garden.

"My favorite job as a teenager was bailing hay. I typically moved (threw) over 20 tons of 40lb bales in a day – I got paid for great outdoor exercise and I slept well at night! Building wooden fences wasn't far behind."

25 Random Things About Me #8. Trip Lucas, Facebook.

The simple farmhouse was built in 1900. To say it needed some modernization is an understatement. Central heat was one of them. The house and kitchen had been somewhat modernized in the 40s when indoor plumbing, an electric range, and asbestos shingles had been added. The kitchen had an electric range but was still heated by a big wood stove. There was a smaller wood stove for heat in the dining room, and there was a fireplace in each of the four bedrooms and the living room. The chimneys had been deemed unsafe at some point and weren't allowed to be used for fires when we bought the place. In the 1940's asbestos shingles, originally thought to be such a good thing, were known to be hazardous to health by the time we came along. Within a year, I had them removed. The house had no insulation in the walls, either. On late summer/early fall weekends, before we moved in, we had family workdays at the house. Going room by room, Joe and nine-year-old Trip took crowbars to the old plaster and wood lathing, removing it all down to the studs. Dusty and eager, the four girls, ages 7(two of them) and 6 (the other two), and I went to work. Looking like a model on a magazine cover, Kate had her long hair covered with a red bandana. Beginning with the upstairs, we girls scooped up the plaster and lathing with shovels and threw it out one of the windows. It went into the bed of a pick-up truck below. Then we did the downstairs rooms. After that, the pros arrived to install insulation, drywall, new plumbing and central heat, kitchen cabinets, and other modernizations.

Upstairs, we had one large bathroom for the five kids to share – along with a resident black snake or two. The snakes lived under the house in summer, but in winter, they came into the house up through the walls to catch mice, eventually shedding their skins next to the water pipes behind the upstairs bathtub. That's where we found the snakeskins each Spring. On the other side of that wall was a small closet in the hall. As Trip grew, he developed a pastime involving the mice. His room was the only one sharing a wall with the bathroom and his door was right next to that hall closet. He would catch a mouse in his wastebasket, play with it, and then let it loose again. I didn't know about that for years – maybe not until Trip told me after he had gone to college.

We moved in on a pouring-down-rain January day. Joe's parents brought dinner our first night – fried chicken. We ate it as we sat at the kitchen table. We looked out through the newly installed picture window at the cold rain beating down on the yard and the horse pastures beyond.

My parents came to see us the following summer. That's when Mother sidled up behind me and whispered in my ear, "I like the Blackwell's place better than yours." Really? Mother's comment was another of what my sisters called her "zingers". They served to instill shame. The Blackwell's was an adjoining farm and house that had, back around Civil War time, been part of the same property as ours. In the next year, my aunt and uncle and a couple who were their friends came to visit. They liked our place and were complimentary about it. That helped to massage the hurt from mother's comment.

———

I think of Dana, who has told me she has terrible regrets over not calling Trip when she thought about it in the days before he died. "Mom, I feel guilty for not calling Trip when I thought of him just a few days before. I would have my hand on the phone and not call him," she said. "Now he is gone."

As people are leaving, there's a wedding party waiting in the wings for us to leave the space. Kate and I load up her car with stuff to take home and go to her house where she's invited family and friends to join us. She's upset that Joe isn't coming over, that he's gone home already after leaving all the boxes of Trip's memorabilia that had been in his care in her car. It felt as if he'd wiped his hands of Trip. And the rest of us.

I want to know why this had to happen. When did it start? Could I have stopped the trajectory that was going this way? Or did I have anything at all to do with how things were going to unfold? Often in my life I had been told that the current mess, whatever it was, was all my fault. Like the night the upstairs pipes froze – and then broke, one unusually freezing and windy winter day back in the 70's. It was not long after I had had the asbestos siding removed from the original wood siding, which turned out to be in quite good shape after over sixty or seventy years, thirty of them under the asbestos. The upright piano in the hall below was ruined. That was the end of Trip's piano lessons after that, even though the piano tuner came several times and pronounced the piano right again. I continued to play, which always made me happy. Trip decided that the piano wasn't his forte when he heard a classmate playing and realized that the boy had a real gift. Neither Trip nor I had the gift for it. Still, we enjoyed learning. I can still read the notes and play the right keys. Making music is something else.

I know every bad thing is not my fault, but losing Trip was a doozy. I am coming to believe that fault is not where the truth is. The truth is where we wrap ourselves and all of life with compassion and kindness, the love that holds it all together. Because stuff happens, no matter what you think or believe. And *why not* me? William Butler Yeats wrote in "Sailing to Byzantium" that each of us is fastened to a dying animal. Maybe it is when we accept that truth that we can also understand that Love *is* what holds it all together. What Trip's friends and his teacher/friend Townley were saying about Trip was that he was wicked smart, compassionate, athletic, fun, and full of life. What a gift he was.

In a month or two, I got a bill for the tech part of the chapel use. It was around $200. If I remember correctly, the chapel itself is free to alumni. I felt disgruntled enough that I just didn't pay the bill until I got a notice that the University would report this to credit agencies, and it might affect my rating. I waited some more until I got a second notice. At that point, I called the treasurer, whose name was on the bill. I was surprised that she answered her phone. I explained to her my reluctance to pay since I didn't feel that I came close to getting anything worth the charges. I told her that I was willing to pay something, but not all of it. She insisted, "No, no," and kindly erased the whole bill and sent me a notice to that effect. I was glad that someone at the auspicious and stately University of Virginia was gracious and had a heart.

My sense of isolation returned, bringing fatigue with it. I had miles left to go. There was to be a celebration of Trip's life in Austin in a month and much to be done. I asked myself why I was doing it and then remembered that it was because so many of Trip's friends in Austin had asked if there would be something there and when.

First, my childhood best friend, Maude, was dying. She'd been through a many-year process of cancer, hope, more cancer, but just before the celebration for Trip in Charlottesville, she sent a text – she could no longer speak due to a total laryngectomy – to say that her caretaker was going to bring her up to Virginia from her home in North Carolina to attend the service, that she felt she must be there. I was surprised and wondered if she truly had the strength to make it. As it turned out, she didn't. She texted to tell me that she was unable to come, having had another medical episode.

In the late afternoon on the day of Trip's service, when family and friends were gathered at Kate's home, I got another message from Maude. She asked me if I would change my flight home and come to North Carolina to see her first. I did. The airline was not the least bit cooperative or generous about the change. They charged $1000.00 because my friend was not a family member. Talk about having no heart. It was almost unbelievable, but I knew I had to go. I did and was there for a few days while she was still in the hospital. I knew I wouldn't make it back again before her death. It turned out to be a very sad ending to a long relationship that went back to two horse-crazy grade-school girls and four self-centered parents who became drinking buddies. Maude and I met on the playground by the monkey bars. Both of us girls were emotionally traumatized by our parents. We supported each other for a long time. After her divorce and move to North Carolina, we somewhat re-connected, but then I moved west. Her health deteriorated probably due to her own bad health habits - a lot of cigarettes - and by the time of her final decline, we were miles and years and habits apart. The original bond was still strong, however, and I couldn't ignore it. I felt sad for her suffering in her last few years. I still think about her kids and exchange Christmas cards with one of them.

I arrived back home and somehow managed to begin thinking about Austin. Why, how, can so many things go wrong at once? I felt old, familiar feelings, telling myself it was my fault, that I'd done life all wrong.

As I write, it is hard to believe I was able to withstand those two events so close together. Truth *is* stranger than fiction. And human resilience is an amazing force. But when did I get to stop holding my breath? I asked myself. The yogis say, "Breathe". It is harder than you think.

Chapter Six

"I have been a proponent of $4 per gallon gas since getting my MBA in '97. I believed that nothing short of this would spur American innovation to create alternatives. In 2008, this belief was proven to be true. Many thought that high fuel prices would destroy the U.S. economy. What was not known was that a ridiculous, unnecessary, multi-trillion-$-total-cost foreign war, dramatically reducing taxes and oversight on the top 1% of the wealthiest (and corporations) while goosing the 'middle' 99% of individuals, and the resultant deficit spending would destroy it first. It was also not foreseen by me that the cost of NOT increasing U.S. gas taxes to get $4/gal gas was continued, and increased funding of the very nations that our self-perpetuating military-industrial complex declared we needed to spend more $ to fight against. A black fly in your chardonnay is NOT ironic; people funding the destruction of 'their' way of life in the name of preserving 'their' way of life is. Everything contains its opposite?"

25 Random Things About Me #24. Trip Lucas, Facebook.

I was just beginning to plan for the Austin, Texas, celebration of Trip's life when I decided to go to my yoga class for the first time since Trip's death over two months earlier. I had a lot of uncertainty about being together enough in both body and spirit. I went and was spreading out my mat, still asking myself if I was enough *in* my body to do this when I sensed Trip's spirit beside me. He was transmitting to me this thought,

"I wonder what it would be like to do yoga without a body?"

That cracked me up. It sounded exactly like something Trip would think and would say. My whole being sighed with relief, and some happy tears leaked out, knowing that Trip *was* with me. It made me happy and able to fully participate in yoga class. The mist of shock, sadness, and loss that had been enveloping me lifted, at least for the class. It also made me think that spirits really *are* here. I've heard it said, "he is still with you", and similar comments, but I had not experienced it like this before now. Except for that morning a day or two after Trip died when he appeared before me, I thought that departed spirits were "here" in our hearts and minds, which they are, but this presence, and actually hearing his voice, was something else. After those two times, I experienced him more often and am now at a place where it isn't something I think could happen; it is something that I know happens.

The Austin celebration was a thing that I felt very pleased about afterwards. Everything about it felt right – the place: Milton Reimers Ranch Park in Dripping Springs, Texas; the setting, which is above several beautiful bends in the Pedernales River; the climbing routes; the people; the caterers, all of it. The people – before Dana and I went there the first time to go through Trip's belongings, she wondered out loud about erecting a bench or some such thing in his memory. It would be near where Trip climbed in Austin. I called his friend, Jeff, who thought it was a great idea. He was the one who wrote to me immediately after Trip's death to say,

"Trip was a special, sensitive man, and we loved him very much."

He said that this park, Milton Reimers Ranch Park in Dripping Springs, had become a central gathering place for the climbers. He contacted some people who were climbing friends, along with a park ranger and maybe another person or two. Some of their names I have forgotten by now, but their kindness still sticks in my memory. They all met Dana and me there, at Reimers. They took us on a walking tour to see some of the climbing routes. At the very last one, one of our guides said, "This is Liposuction (climbers must have contests for quirky route names). It's one of the ones that Trip climbed the day before he died." It's well-named. It looks like a huge open maw.

We talked about where we might put a bench and decided what we might use for a bench. There was the idea of using a boulder that was already somewhere in the park and where and how we'd find it. The Park has boulders all over it. These climbing friends of Trip's, who were complete strangers to Dana and me, welcomed us and helped us do whatever we wanted. It felt as if we had known them forever. Maybe that's just who they are, and it is how they would be with any family of a lost member of their climbing group. Whatever the reason, I was and am still grateful and will remember them for the rest of my life.

In the space of an afternoon, we had hashed out a preliminary plan. Two of them were going to scour the park for suitable big rocks/boulders that could be dragged, with the help of some heavy equipment, to the area we picked. They suggested that near the top of a climb named Prototype Wall was a good spot. It is where climbers would finish the climb up and could sit to rest while enjoying the lovely river overlook. I can't believe that it only took a month for those climbing friends of Trip's to find the right boulder, get it moved, and more. Meanwhile, Dana's friend Sean from an earlier part of her life lived in the area and had found for us the place that could make the bronze memorial plaque to attach to the rock bench and I engaged them to make it.

One of the climbers sent me a video of Trip "sending" (climber lingo) a climb one day. What a treasure to have that, seeing Trip in action on a climb and hearing his voice making comments and small talk as he went. That's the one and only voice memo that I have. It warms my heart like nothing else. I live with competing emotions of loss/sadness and gratitude for how all those people helped and gave up their time. Looking back on that time, I have the sense of being outside myself, watching me go through the motions as if I am a stranger to myself.

Again, there were caterers to be discovered and contacted. The best one turned out to be Whole Foods. Its headquarters is in Austin. It's ironic that even though Trip didn't like their prices and refused to shop there, I found that they could offer the best good food. And they were easy to deal with. Sorry, Trip.

For the Austin memorial, the climbers' parking lot has a small pavilion where we gathered informally and talked about Trip. Again, a few friends of Trip's – three of them climbers – have some prepared thoughts to share about Trip. Jeff, a writer by profession, had warm and funny things to share, including a story about the day they met at a gathering after a climb. He told us, "My first impression of Trip was that he was very well-read, and I thought it was unique that he said he never passed up a body of water without swimming in it."

It's true, as Jeff said, that trip was well-read. From early on until he died, he was a devoted reader. He was always a hare, not a tortoise, in that he would go full speed for a few days, no matter the venue – be it school or playtime or sports – and then he would wind up in his bed kicked back and reading for days at a time (not skipping school, of course). He read voraciously and widely, and for some reason, that touched me, the part of me that could relate. Most of all, I think it always warmed my heart that he felt so free to be himself.

He wasn't inhibited like I had been as a kid. I always felt as if my parents were looking over my shoulder, judging everything I did and what I said. They were judging all the time. When I was in a horse show, my father never missed a chance to find some little mistake that, according to him, I made and to comment on it in a way that made me feel inadequate. "Didn't you feel that?" he would say. From the vantage point of my years now, I realize that things have changed in terms of how to ride horses that went over fences since Daddy had ridden in shows and competed. I had read about and adopted a newer, more humane, and enlightened way of being on a horse's back. Because of that sea change, saddles were also different, kinder to the horse and lighter. My father never acknowledged the change that I had learned or that I was riding a different version of horses over fences. I was riding in Hunter's classes. Daddy rode open jumpers. There's a world of difference in what's expected and what you see and feel. In addition, there were a lot of years between his time in the show ring and mine. He was living in the past and would only be happy if I could reprise it for him. I couldn't and didn't.

My mother did something equally critical regarding several things about me, but what I chose to read is a tad ironic. Mother was a pseudo-intellectual. My reading material was never highbrow enough for her. Yet, which of us read Les Misérables in toto? In high school, no less. Because I wanted to, not because it was required reading. When I was in high school tennis matches, there was a particular opponent from another school who intimidated me on the tennis court with her gum-chewing nonchalance and what felt like an attitude of superiority to me. Her mother was always with her, too. Mother could not resist telling me that I should beat that girl. And how. Mother, who played tennis but was just an average country club player, felt entitled enough to be the expert and to pass on to me her need to have me win over my opponent. I kind of liked my opponent. What made it hard for me in that case was mother's need to have me win. And in Daddy's case it was his need to see me doing things exactly like he had. My parents were difficult and hurtful. If you read any of the Harry Potter books, you might remember the dementors. They are dark creatures that consume human happiness, creating an ambiance of coldness, darkness, misery, and despair. They drain happiness and hope from humans. That is a good description of my parents. Not only did they do those things the dementors did, but they also made us children feel as if we were bad people and unworthy of anything good.

One thing I've come to believe as I've been writing is that my parents had what the DSM (Diagnostic and Statistical Manual of Mental Disorders) calls Personality Disorders. I have had experience both in my training years and in my years as a psychotherapist with people who have Personality Disorders. I think each of my parents had one or two. Narcissistic Personality Disorder was one of them. In mother's case, I think she also had Borderline Personality Disorder. In layman's terms, my parents came across as spoiled brats. They had good and loving parents who probably did not truly spoil them. I think my parents spoiled themselves their whole lives together. They were self-indulgent, self-important, self-centered heavy drinkers together. As far as I can tell, they were unaware of their effect on their daughters. There's one thing for which I will be eternally grateful. I am glad my parents were gone when Trip took his life. The shame and degradation they would have unleashed on Trip and me, along with whoever they deemed deserved it, would have been ugly and hurtful. For Daddy, there would have been his Catholic disapproval and judgment. I am sure of that. During my pregnancy with Carter and Dana, I told my parents that I was going to have my tubes tied after that. Daddy said to me that I should consult a priest and that I would feel better if I got permission. To me, that is an example of his being a rule follower, no matter if the rules made sense to you or not.

——

After the talks, we took a short walk across a scrubby Texas field to dedicate the rock that will be used as the bench marked in memory of Trip. We were warned about short but sneaky prickly things on the ground that could easily stab us. I saw them as we walked.

On the boulder/bench, we will put a bronze plaque with a bas relief from a photo of Trip climbing a route on it and the dates of his birth and death, with the exhortation "climb on" - Kate's idea. The manufacturer couldn't have it ready in time, but we had a photo of it for all of us to see. So many contributed to this bench, from providing the idea to finding the suitable rock to hauling it there to finding the place to create the plaque, to donations, to finally placing the plaque, which one of the climbers did when the plaque was ready. They consisted of Trip's climbing community and friends, three of his sisters, park workers, and others.

At the dedication of the bench, quite a few stayed a good while after. Several people took handfuls of Trip's ashes and tossed them toward the river or just down over the climbing area. We took pictures of us, the family that was present, which consisted of Antoinette, Kate, Dana, my sister Auntoinette's two, Kee and John, and me. Topper and his wife, Barry, were there, too. Topper has been like family since I was young. Dana's friend, Sean, and his Laura were there. It seemed as if we and Trip's many friends had become friends, and soon, the picture-taking included all of us in various combinations. It could have been a wedding or Christmas it was that congenial. As the sun wase getting lower in the sky, we gradually walked back to the pavilion in little bunches, and some left. Trip's Laura had been in attendance, but she left before we walked out to see the bench. Someone in the group suggested stopping for dinner on the way back into Austin.

After some discussion, we wound up at a roadside diner. It was dark outside as we found newly familiar faces and picked our way through the gravel parking lot, looking for the entrance. In my memory, the diner appeared to be built higgledy-piggledy, á la the house that Jack built, because of its many physically and decoratively unrelated parts, as if they had been built little by little. I started to feel a bit tired, separate from, and just watching, everyone else, but I was carried along by the energy stream of the group.

The next day, I went to Topper and Barry's to deposit some of Trip's ashes in a small garden plot. It overlooked Lake Austin. Barry and Topper had been home away from home for Trip, his sisters, his girlfriend Laura, and before that, Trip and his wife, Kim.

I felt strangely detached from something in me. Something that wanted connection, warmth, wholeness, and love. That yearned for Trip to still be alive. And more. I don't know what that more was. But it felt as if I'd lost a limb. A hold. Like a climbing hold. I couldn't cry about it, either. It feels now, a few years later, as if it is something that had always been missing for me. I think now, it was a connection with myself. The real me, the one that hides, or did for a long time.

Several years before this, I went to Austin to see Trip and Kim. Before I went, I asked Trip if he'd take me rock climbing. He took me to a place on the outskirts of Austin where other newbies were also learning. Some were in one area learning how to "boulder". It seemed a lot was going on, but it wasn't crowded and felt collegial. Trip fitted the harness on me for the first time ever. That's when I understood how, with Trip holding one end of a rope, if I started to fall, he could stop me. Wow. That's a big responsibility and brings tears to my eyes as I write that he did that. Rock climbers do that. Some don't, the free climbers and others, but they are the mega ones.

For me, the most dear and memorable part of it was a moment when I was maybe half-way up the 35' natural rock wall and stuck, with both hands and both legs spread out wide. I had no idea where to go next. I remember a slender sapling being a little to my right and close to the wall, so I couldn't see very clearly what was in that direction. I had no idea what to do. That's when Trip, who was below and chatting with a friend who was there helping another climber, noticed me and said, "Mom, I'm not supposed to tell you what to do because figuring it out is part of it, but if you put your left foot under your right arm, I think you will find a way."

I looked, and there was a hold right over there. I put my left foot just like Trip said, reached the hold, and everything after that revealed itself to me. Wow! Talk about being pumped. The next thing I remember after that was being all the way at the top and looking out over the almost level surface there, thinking, "wow, look at me! Look at this. Here I am at the top. I climbed up here." Trip was still married to Kim at the time. I was divorced and had my psychotherapy practice up and running, so it was after 1995 by a year or more. I've never forgotten that feeling of exhilaration and accomplishment and of being helped by Trip. He *was* a good teacher. I felt safe with him.

I miss him as I write. I miss him a lot. Yesterday, when I was sitting in meditation, I felt a presence right beside me. It felt like Trip. It was his energy, his presence.

Chapter Seven

I can sew my own clothes. I am still looking to learn more. I'm not into sewing; I just like clothes that fit. At 5'8", I am within one or two inches of the average male height – shouldn't half the clothing be made for smaller people instead of being nearly impossible to find? Shouldn't 30" waist 30" pant length be normal based on Vitruvian man proportions – instead of at the smallest, hard-to-find, end of the clothing spectrum?

25 Random Things About Me #11. Trip Lucas, Facebook.

I'm an ENTP, but I'm borderline E/I and T/F on the Myers-Briggs scale.

 25 Random Things About Me #14. Trip Lucas, Facebook.

I agree with Trip. I think he was equally an F and a T in the Myers-Briggs classification.

After Austin and the second celebration, I was depleted. Grief exhausted me, and making sense of Trip's loss was even more exhausting. It felt impenetrable, a mystery, and not one that I thought would be revealed any time soon. It isn't as if I came home and spent all my waking hours thinking about Trip, but it was a kind of vapor that trailed me and, at times, surrounded me. I didn't always realize it was happening, either, except in retrospect. I wouldn't remember what someone said or did not realize that I was not completely in the moment until something happened that got my attention. I seemed to have let go of most of the shock and anger I had felt earlier. But the authentic sadness and loss were just setting in. Acceptance? Not so much.

Physical exertion and nature are two things that have always helped to bring me into myself in a healthy way and grounded me. I have enjoyed both all my life, both during and after mucking manure out of horse stalls, riding a horse out in nature – the woods nearby for example - weeding, tennis, or skiing. Jogging is a strange phenomenon in that in all the 27 or 28 years that I did it six days a week; I was both here in the moment jogging down the street, but also in another zone. It was a zone of ease and openness when answers to questions or new ideas would pop into my head. Nothing bothered me; all was possible.

But Trip died, and I was not grounded by exertion. It was the pain. I'd never been there before, having that kind of pain. I'd had plenty of emotional pain, but his loss hurt in a depth of my being that astonished me. To have known that delightful, unique person since he was in my womb, to give birth to him, watch him grow, to know the man he became meant I assumed he would be here after I was gone. In fact, in his last year or two, we had discussed my end-of-life plans and what I'd like for a service or celebration. Trip even asked what songs I picked. Music was important to him. When I told him there was a specific item that I wanted him to have, a pin that I had turned into a pendant. He said he'd like that and that he was sentimental about it. At his three-year-old Christmas, he had been asked to pick one of six wrapped boxes that would be mine, and the one he picked had had that gift in it. It is a pretty, older piece of gold with some gems set in it. It was given by my bachelor uncle, one of six different things he gave to his six nieces over six years. One or two were family pieces. The rest were ones he purchased to have something for each of us. But now, at this point after Trip's death, I realized that Trip would not be here after I am gone. I was lost, not sure where I belonged or who that pendant should go to now.

I kept asking myself why he took his life, what was it in him that pushed him that far over the edge. I blamed myself, then I blamed Joe – in my mind, not to his face. Trip did tell me once in one of his last years that he didn't think he had much guidance growing up. I thought there was truth to that. He and his sisters were good kids, so we didn't have to lean on them because of behavior, honesty, kindness, or consideration for others, but we might have extended ourselves to talk more about how to live life, make decisions, and more with them. How to think about life. How they might want to live it. How to trust yourself in making decisions (something it has taken me decades to get halfway there). To be intentional about the human beings they became. After that train of thought, I flailed around a while longer, looking for an explanation. Trip did have some mentors who were either teachers or, in the case of at least one, a family friend who really cared for Trip, Peter, and who provided some guidance. He had so much in terms of ability, personality, and looks. His looks - chiseled face, lean, strong physique – were one thing. But his smiling eyes, often with a hint of mischief about to happen, made him approachable, along with a look of kindness and sensitivity. He was smart and physically gifted, fun, with lots of friends. He did have a deeply thoughtful and kind personality. Like many of us, there's an inner quality that we don't share with others, but it is there. I imagine that it was some intensity, the part that caused him to want to always do his best, not for anyone else, but because he wanted it, as his teacher in grade school wrote about him. I will always remember the photo of him at his St. Christopher's graduation. He looked serious and deep in thought. You would think it would be a happy day. But during that senior year, he had asked me why he – or anyone - should go to college. There was something about that passage for him. He took it as a decision he needed to make for himself, not go to college just because it was an expected next step. I liked that about him.

As I write, I am aware of the unconsciously intense moment that those passages were in my own life for me. Each graduation - high school, undergrad, and grad school must have contained anxiety for me. I think so because, for each one, I put on a few pounds. I was padding my anxiety with food, mostly sugar. In my conscious mind, I was unaware of being nervous about the upcoming passage. My unconscious was registering my concern about overeating. Then, I'd have to undo the effects. Why didn't I speak up when it was happening to Trip? There it is again – the fear of my own knowing, a lack of trust in myself. There were – and are – times that I think something I can't explain is a mystery that shall be revealed, and I just wait for it to appear vs. asking questions. Now, at this age, I am pretty sure that for me my hesitation in my own life had to do with not feeling as if anyone had my back. I certainly didn't know how to back me up. Sometimes, it was very hard for me to handle living that way. At least at those points in my life. As for Trip back then, maybe it was something similar. I think he wanted his father's guidance or affirmation. I don't know. He knew he had mine, but I'm not sure he felt that he had his father's love and support.

Trip was more than capable in all areas of his life, but I saw him the time two years before he died when he and Laura moved to England for yet another of the six-month contract software jobs. He was on edge, nervous about what looked to me like performance anxiety. When they were getting ready to go, Trip told Laura that her job when they went was to take care of him. I had never seen him that anxious. Maybe about impending tests or exams, but because he was a good student, excellent in most things, I always knew he'd do well. I didn't worry, but he must have. He expected the best from himself. But we all need encouragement and empathy along with discernment as we work to be our best. Maybe that's where I failed him, or both of us parents failed him.

For sure, my parents did not encourage or advise us. Quite the opposite. They lectured, belittled, and *dis*couraged. Daddy was loud, pompous, and demanding. He stomped through the house when he left each morning, often slamming doors as he went. He was loud and scary when he lost his temper, which was often. Mother was down and dirty, sneaky with her personal critiques. Always shaming. Before I left home for college, there were several times that I was going out either to a party or preparing for something special, and Mother would say, "be yourself". Every time she said that I would think to myself, "I don't know who that is." I think when we are young, we see ourselves via the looks on our parents' faces and in their eyes. I did. I saw incompetence and disapproval. Or, maybe, as in my father's last words, "I am SO disappointed in you."

"Nice people, don't do that," Mother would say about something I had just done as if I weren't nice people. Bessel Van der Kolk says in his book <u>The Body Keeps the Score</u>: "If your parents' faces never lit up when they looked at you, it's hard to know what it feels like to be loved and cherished." I did not know what it felt like to be loved and cherished by my parents. I will say that my grandparents' faces lit up when they saw me. Is that what held Trip back? I know he knew that I loved and cherished him, but perhaps I wasn't enough. I am also pretty sure that *he* loved his parents, his sisters, and grandparents.

Over a month after my return from Austin, I went to Virginia to be with my daughters for Christmas. When I came back, I did what I had to for my volunteer job at the international alpine ski race that was in early February, four months since Trip's death. Preparation consumed the whole Vail community because the entire ski world would be here. "2015!" signs were up, with bumper stickers everywhere. My heart was not in it, but I went through the motions.

I tried to ignore the toll that loss and grief were taking on me. It was that hiding part of me. Or the denial that I was still capable of invoking at times, that I learned at my mother's knee.

"Want to come ski with us?" my ski-locker mate and her boyfriend asked me.

"Ok", I said, pushing aside my uncertainty and the fact that my body still felt a million miles away from me. Now, I might have enough courage, the courage to be me, to say that I'm not ready yet. But I didn't then. Or, at least, I couldn't refrain from people-pleasing even then.

They headed for an area that is not my favorite. I hesitated but went anyway. I was about halfway down when I did something wrong and fell in an awkward position: legs spread out, upper body downhill, my skis had not been released, and one ankle hurt. My ski day was over, my ankle broken – not a bad break, but enough to keep me off skis for the next several weeks. My body had been keeping the score of my emotional well-being, and of course, it was non-existent. Trip was gone, the memorials done, but I was not over his loss or my grief. Lots of healing still had to happen, but I was letting others' well-meaning push me out of my need to continue to grieve and to listen to my body. If I had been my therapy client, I would have reminded myself that it takes as long as it takes. I had been having some *"why me?"*. Later, when I was getting better, I began to think, *"why not me?"*

By this time, I allowed my mind to slow down to the level where I could just *be*. Grief colored the background, a kind of no-color shade, but I was less able to think about that or make sense of anything except the immediate requirements of getting through my days. Maybe that was a blessing. I didn't come up for air or take deep breaths for months. I re-read cards, notes, and emails from my friends and Trip's friends following his death. That prompted me to write them notes to acknowledge their thoughtfulness. With each one, I saw and felt human connections, kindness, and so much more. It was a slow process. Some days I got little done and was lost in sadness as well as gratitude for the people, for love. I went over and over many of the moments of that September 10. It's ironic that September 10th was my parents' anniversary. Two awful things on the same date.

In May, I started to think that it was time to have some sort of renewal, to start to tune into something healing. I went to a meditation retreat led by an American Buddhist monk who led the first such retreat I went to, which had been enlightening and helpful. Not this one. It was a colossal disappointment. The man had changed or forgotten his mission. I left early, glad to be out of there.

Part of what was churning within me was a desire to do *something* as a memorial to Trip and who he was in his life. There was the idea of writing a book, but that was the most daunting thought I'd had in years. I love to read and to write, but just for me. For decades, I had written something – daily journal, little stories, poems, a column here and there - but did not believe in my ability. That disbelief began when I was eight. I had decided I would write a book, my own version of Little House on the Prairie. My third-grade teacher, Mrs. Black, had been reading the book to us in class. Mrs. Black with her very black hair, thick black eyebrows, and black stiletto heels. I was enchanted by the story – a bit overwhelmed by Mrs. Black. She looked a little like one of the nefarious women in the Dick Tracy comics, right down to pointy bosoms. The evil women always had pointy breasts and angular faces; the good women had rounded ones. I sat down at the small drop-front wooden desk Santa had brought me for Christmas. I had rustled up a yellow legal pad, probably from my lawyer grandfather, Gigi, picked up a pencil and began. It didn't take long before Mother looked over my shoulder to see what I'd written. She quickly squashed my initiative by saying,

"You shouldn't use *that* word!"

I was crushed, devastated. The word was about the mother in my story. I had written that she "yelled" up the stairs to someone. Of course, Mother didn't want to be seen as *that* mother. She would never do something so unladylike and socially inappropriate as to yell. I was engulfed in the mortification of being criticized by Mother. And I couldn't understand it from any perspective but that of my eight-year-old self, especially for something that was so exciting and calling to me. I put down my pencil and yellow legal pad for years. In the decades after, I had seldom screwed up the courage to give her – the mother in my head - a challenge. The attempts that I had made to unseat her from her throne in my psyche had been short-lived, and they hadn't taken away my characterization of being *unworthy* or *incapable*. They included talks composed and given for class assignments (which were good), even one or two several-week writing classes.

In addition to mother's criticism, Mrs. Black had shamed me in front of the whole class by saying something totally untrue. She had given the class time to read on our own –my version of heaven – and right in the middle, she called out that "some people aren't really reading, but just moving their eyes across the page, and "MaryLamb Bond, you are one of them!" I was mortified. Again. Of course, I was reading. I *loved* to read. I could not tell my parents about this event. They would have made me feel worse and shamed me. They always took the side of the authority. That did it for my third-grade year, as far as I was concerned. I faked being sick and anything else I could to get out of school the rest of that year. So much so that, of course, Mother took me to the doctor, assuming I had something seriously medical. Neither she nor Doctor Basman thought to ask if anything was wrong at school. I faked it the whole way, but I am pretty sure Mrs. Black knew I was, which no doubt did nothing to change the dark and wrong judgment she had visited on me. In my memory, she's a very dark black.

At this place since Trip's death, a little voice was pushing me, pushing me. It would pop out from behind where it hid and whisper to me, "what about a book?" it would say. "Go away", I'd say. As I wrote that, I was astounded at how I had regressed in my psychological growth after Trip's death.

Sometimes, something I least expected would come along and nudge my fear away. Something like remembering the story of Jane Doe. Jane Doe was a deer who was found by friends and country neighbors we had. They lived on a large family farm and had developed the practice of rescuing abandoned fawns, caring for them and releasing them into the wild. They were successful in all cases except for one, the fawn they named Jane Doe, but whom they nicknamed *Itty* because she was so itty bitty when rescued. At first, she had to stay in the couple's bathroom for the wife, Francie, to hand feed her through her first many nights. Then she went to an enclosure where each fawn went until his or her release. Itty didn't release well because even though she adapted to the wild and had her herd of deer, she kept returning to her human family to visit, walking right into the house where she had been cared for as a fawn and demanding ginger snaps. Francie thinks her children may have played with Itty too much. After eight years of this released doe, going out but returning for her visits, one evening she appeared in the yard very sick. Francie called one of the local horse vets who looked at Itty but was not sure what was wrong. He gave her penicillin and propped her up between two hay bales so she could breathe more easily. He hoped she would be better by morning. Francie says they set up two-hour checks on Itty during the night. Francie had the 2 AM check and found Itty to be looking a little brighter but still down. She gave her some water and re-propped her with the hay. Then she sat there stroking Itty's head. Francie says that Itty,

"Put her head in my lap and took her last breath with a sigh and no struggle for breath.

As I sat there in the moonlight, crying and reminiscing about her as a fawn, a cloud came over the moon, and it grew dark. A few minutes later, the cloud cover blew over, and in this misty moment, I thought I was seeing things because in a semi-circle around us, I could make out a herd of 8 or so does. I was scared to move, thinking it was a mirage. But it was not. The moon disappeared again and again, and the clouds would disperse, but the image was always the same: misty but clear. Itty's herd was there around us, twitching their ears and looking right at us. It was magical and a beautiful end to her life. I sat there for probably an hour with her, and slowly, they left quietly and one at a time and disappeared into the night. The whole experience left me awed and breathless, as you can imagine. I will never forget it."

~ Francie S.A. Reed, with her permission

Nor will I forget. Remembering the sweet story of Jane Doe restored my belief that in all of nature, it is important to honor a life that has ended, especially the life of my son. No matter how it is done.

Chapter Eight

Forgiving others and myself is probably the hardest thing I've ever learned to do – and I still can't do it very well. Hmmmm.

25 Random Things About Me #13. Trip Lucas, Facebook.

Swiss Psychiatrist Carl Jung had several theories. One of them he called Individuation.

It was his nomenclature for a process of higher self-development that was the goal of the philosophical alchemists of antiquity. Another definition, from Jung, is that it is a "lifelong project of becoming more nearly the whole person we were meant to be, as intended by a reliable *inner* source, … not what parents or an inflated ego would expect."

I've been told that "figure out who you are and do it on purpose" is Dolly Parton's version. I have an Oprah Winfrey quote on a magnet: "The whole point of being alive is to evolve into the complete person you were intended to be." I think all are saying that we already *are* who we are, but we may not be fully embracing - or living - *whoever* that is. Often, there are obstacles, both within and without, that must be surmounted. Fear is one of them. In my case, it is fear of so many things that have to do with psychological and personal growth. Taking a chance on me has been just plain scary. Stay-hidden-in-the-closet scary. I literally used to hide in my long, narrow closet when I was young and either Mother or Daddy, or both, were in a bad temper. The floor was raised at the end of the closet under the closet rod, which made for a little step back there in the back. It was away from the door and the light that came through under the door. I would sit on the step and feel safe in the almost invisible, dark space.

My first step into mental health involved attending Al-Anon, which is a spin-off of Alcoholics Anonymous. Al-Anon is for family and friends of alcoholics. After Mother had her melt-down and cry for help, she began to attend Al-Anon meetings at the urging of her psychiatrist. I think their internist encouraged both of my parents to attend the 12-step programs. Mother saw Daddy as the sick one and herself as the victim. She never admitted that she, too, had an alcohol addiction. Or that she might be just as sick. Nevertheless, she urged me and my sisters to join Al-Anon. We did. All three of us.

I'll never forget Daddy, red-faced, shouting, and walking alongside me as I was backing my car around to head out of my parents' driveway, saying, "I can do my own program!" that was soon after Mother's meltdown and psychiatric care. He meant as opposed to the AA program of recovery. He never did get into recovery. Neither did Mother. She did go to Al-Anon, which was about her response to Daddy's alcoholism. Related. Not the same thing.

When I began to attend those meetings, I became aware of the co-dependent thinking of me and many of those in Al-Anon. It lacked clarity and good judgment. Instead, I noticed that many co-dependents tried to control everything around them as their way of dealing with the dysfunctional lives they were living. They were the ones who would take over the meetings. One even went so far as to print out all the rules we should adhere to in the meetings I attended in Richmond – no cross-talking, for example - and she came to meetings armed with her loose-leaf notebook full of them. She was also the timekeeper. My sisters told me that mother was one of those types. She was so controlling that she was responsible for a lot of new meetings that were started by those who fled mother.

The other kind of co-dependents were the ones who did not assert themselves but avoided conflict above all else and were resentful and ineffective. Some just made excuses for the way things were without making any changes whatsoever. I learned a lot, most of it about how I could stop being a victim and help myself to grow. I began my habits of reflection and journaling during that time.

Mornings were hectic at home with everyone else, Joe and the five kids, needing to get dressed, eat breakfast, and leave for school and work by 7 or 7:30. I was the slow poke. I have never been one of those people who jumps out of bed with great alacrity, ready to function at my peak. Even though I am an early bird, I tend to gradually awake, putter around, and very slowly enter the world of wakefulness and readiness. That made me the least efficient factor in the morning. I tried, but I was muddled and not good at it. I give Al-Anon and its readings credit for spurring me to get up at 5 AM and go to the kitchen for quiet time. A cup or two of tea, a reading or two, some journaling and in time, I began to be fully awake and much better at helping everyone else get breakfast and out the door. I had begun a series of changes in me. I was 39. That was the same year that I had the revelation at the stoplight. That was the moment that really set me on my journey. Mary Oliver's poem, The Journey, is about the journey each one of us must take.

My Al-Anon phase of growth included yet another one. It was serendipitous that a local artist, Nancy Witt, whose art intrigued me, was instrumental in forming the group in Richmond that studied the work and life of the late Swiss psychiatrist Carl G. Jung. I had some like-minded friends in a book discussion group I had joined. I also joined Jungian Venture, which was formed to study the work of Carl Jung. That opened worlds inside me that I hadn't known were there, nor had I, early on, the words to describe them. Jung thought that the unconscious in a person's psyche was important to understanding the person. He had been a pupil of Freud but went beyond Freud in his thinking about the unconscious and the human psyche. For example, in the unconscious is the shadow, both the dark one and there can be a bright one, too. He believed that dreams were "the royal road to the unconscious". Therefore, his work with patients involved paying attention to and interpreting their dreams, the night-time ones, not the aspirational ones. I had been paying attention to and remembering my dreams. Then, I formed the habit of recording them. Learning about their meaning and interpretation was, and still is, enlightening and inspiring to me. When clients come to me with dreams, I take that as an invitation to help them understand their dreams in a psychological and symbolic way.

During the time I was learning, I had a disturbing dream in which people I knew were hunting me down and threatening me. One or two of them had weapons in their hands. That led me to a Jungian-oriented therapist who proved invaluable in helping me interpret the meaning of my dreams. She believed in helping people explore their creativity, too. Because of her, I began to get re-acquainted with my writer self. I had already been recording my dreams, writing in my journal, and, in a short time, practicing yoga and meditating daily. It wasn't long before I began to leave organized religion and the dogmas that went with it. That was something I had wanted to do for many years but was shy about making the move. I was changing, little by little. My daughter, Dana, says she remembers when I started to change. I also began to write again.

Years before, I changed, when I was still quite young – 11 or 12 - but after my early book attempt, I had asked Mother to show me how she arranged flowers. Her reply? "You're not creative." For a long time, I believed her.

Fast forward a decade after the stoplight moment, two friends decided to celebrate their 50th birthdays by having an event at the Women's Resource Center in Richmond. They invited a woman Jungian Analyst to do a drumming for a group of their friends. To begin, we were told to lie down on the floor and close our eyes. When the drumming began, we were to go somewhere in our imaginations and at some point, we would meet someone on that journey. When we did, we were to ask the person for our wisdom. I could see that this was to be a creative undertaking. It raised my long-held fear that I would not be able to go beyond Mother's condemning statement about my creativity. I was still under Mother's spell and believed all the belittling things she had told me about me. I began the drumming journey with low expectations. In spite of those expectations, I journeyed to a place I had never seen. It started on a winding and dusty red dirt road where I walked until I came to one end of a three-or-four-story adobe building. It looked native American. At ground level, there was a doorway. It led down into a circular room where there was a fire burning in a primitive open fireplace. Across from the fireplace, up high on the wall, was a small window. There were benches in a semi-circle facing the fire and on one of the benches was a wizened old native woman who was facing the fire and smoking a pipe. With my heart pounding loudly in keeping with the drumbeats, I approached the woman, sat down beside her, and asked her for my wisdom. She told me no that I wasn't ready yet. Still, I was thrilled to have gone that far. I went somewhere. I met someone.

About a year later, I drove west with a Virginia friend who had lived in Corrales, New Mexico, just outside of Albuquerque, for several years. We went there and then to Santa Fe. We were on our way, in Trip's well-worn Jeep, to deposit the Jeep with Trip at the Army's Defense Language Institute in Monterey, California. Looking a bit like the Beverly Hillbillies, we were also toting a bed on top of the Jeep for my friend's daughter, who lived with her Navy pilot husband just outside of LA in Oxnard.

On the way to Santa Fe, we stopped at Pecos National Monument, where there is a reconstructed adobe settlement. There, I saw in the flesh a circular room exactly like the one I had visited in that drumming. It is called a Kiva. That was a spiritual and psychological affirmation of something within me. Internally, I grew a few leaps and bounds. When I looked up Kiva, I read that it was a subterranean, often circular, room used by Puebloans and Hopi for spiritual ceremonies. There's a history of there being such rooms, at first not circular, going quite a long time back. The experience confirms Carl Jung's belief about the presence in each person's unconscious of myths and archetypes from all cultures. He believed we were all connected through what he called the "collective unconscious". And there had also been my stoplight experience in which I saw the interconnectedness of everything. Both are an illustration of Jung's idea of connectedness through the Collective Unconscious. It's interesting to me that he once made the remark that Americans would need to get in touch with their native American roots to fully integrate themselves with their land and to fulfill the high ideals of their government. Hmmm.

At this point, since Trip's death, it was the first summer since that awful day. I was still trying to get my bearings and still trying to conjure up something to honor Trip. It was just out of my reach, whatever it was. At least the reach of my everyday self, but there was a part of me, an inner source, that was pushing me. It was causing my fear to rear its head big time. I conflicted with that source. It said to write a book. My ego, or the self I thought I should *appear* to be, was scared to death to do that. The fear was all about failure, plus mother's comment about my creativity, and nothing to do with the psychological necessity of taking the risk.

I took more time doing nothing besides thinking about putting words on the page. On that New Year's Eve, over a year after Trip's death, I was introduced to a woman at a party. "I'm a writer who helps other people get their books written", she said. We talked about writing. Meeting her encouraged me to get started. What I wrote was terrible. Then, from her, I learned the name of another writer who was said to be a good teacher. She suggested I go to one of the teacher's workshops.

I went to a writing conference with a good teacher/writer and later to one of her workshops. At the conference, she gave us some writing prompts. For one of them, I wrote a poem. For some reason, it surprised me more than at other times when I had written something from a prompt. At that moment, I was happy with myself. The teacher inspired me and continues to.

From that point, I began the many drafts between then and now. I slowly realized that the effort fed my soul in a deep way and that writing was what I had always done to make sense of things. Maybe that is what I was meant to do. Several friends remarked that it must be cathartic to be remembering my son in this way. It was. It is. But it was, and is, much more than that. I was fulfilling a lifelong passion for writing and defying Mother's intimidation. It was as if Rumplestiltskin of the Grimm's fairytale by that name had *already* taken my firstborn and I *still* had to spin the straw into, not gold as in the fairy tale, but a book.

I don't think I will ever get over missing Trip's energy, curiosity, creativity, smarts, and fun. His Wisdom. He was interested in and well-read on so many subjects that I can't think of a conversation with him that wasn't interesting, enlightening, or fulfilling in some way. When Trip brought Laura to visit me for the first time, we talked about Trip. One of the things we both appreciated was his creativity. It was as if he saw life from so many angles and could come up with ideas that would bring out something unusual in an every-day object or event. I believe that curiosity and creativity are two of the best traits a person can have.

When Trip was still living at home, an old, no longer used dinner table that had been in our hayloft was outside beside one end of our dairy cow-barn-turned-horse-stable, awaiting removal. That sparked a scene in Trip's mind. He set the table with a placemat, dinnerware, a plate, and a napkin, put a tie on his shirtless torso, and a big white towel-cum-napkin around the neck of Antoinette's pony, Honor Bright (Brighty). Trip pulled up a chair at his place setting. Brighty stood beside him with her nose in a bucket of oats. Antoinette was the photographer. I put that photo in the slideshow. It brought a laugh.

In the process of excavating into Trip's life/my life, which had intertwined ever since before he was born and are continuing after his death, I was feeling the devastating experience of his loss while also trying to get back some of my own equilibrium. In the process, I discovered journals/diaries that Trip kept at UVA. I felt almost as if I shouldn't be reading what he wrote just for himself, but of course, I did read. I was moved by his total honesty with himself in the journals and, at the same time, how he poked fun at himself. One of his entries is about having run over a squirrel with his bike. I was a bit awed over that because I did the exact same thing a few years after he had! I did it on one of my trips to California. We both felt shocked and terrible about it. The squirrels had darted in their squirrely way right under our bikes and then what do you do? It was over in such a flash for both. Trip wanted to put something on his bike to remember the squirrel: a squirrel sticker with an X drawn through it. I didn't get that far, but I did have the inclination to do *some*thing.

I had a related incident recently when I discovered I had trapped a vole in my house's crawl space using one of those glue traps I bought at the grocery store – it was the only kind available at the time. The little thing was still alive and squeaked several small squeaks as I was holding it, trying to decide what to do. I could not try as I might, get it unstuck. Finally, I put it out of its misery, feeling terrible, a murderer. That's the most awful, inhumane kind of trap that I will never, ever use again. RIP Little Vole.

In Trip's journals, he writes about his classes and about girls, of course. At times, he gets philosophical about life and about his intentions for himself, particularly during his time in France. I wish he had continued to write during his life after undergrad and grad school. Trip asked himself about his feelings for certain girls and, once, about which to choose between two of them. Nothing he wrote shocked me or disturbed me; it just made me wish he were still alive. His writing and way of expressing himself is a kind of balm for me. I can hear him saying those words and feel as if I am with him as I read. I am glad that he kept a journal. I miss him.

The hardest part for me is how to go on with my own life. I wonder how I will ever be able to let go of not being able to stop Trip. Before, I felt less than bad about myself because of the shaming ways of my parents that had wormed themselves into my psyche and my whole being, but now, this seems worse. I can't bring Trip back to life. The love I have for him still exists. It always will.

A grad school professor once asked me why I wanted to become a therapist. I said because of my own woundedness. I did not want anyone to ever feel as bad about themselves as I had. Now, I am finding that I can let myself seriously dislike but also detach from who my parents were and, how they treated me and my sisters, how they projected their own fears, needs, and more on to us. The more that I do, the more detached I feel and the more I realize that who they were and what they said is no reflection of me. I can stop taking their actions and words personally. I know that I did not deserve them. A cousin once said to me about my parents, "Those two deserve each other." Maybe so, but *we,* my sisters and I didn't deserve *them.* We didn't deserve to get so fucked up by them.

I have spent a lot of time wondering how and why they would say things to me about me that were not true. How could they *say* such things? Mother would accuse me of things I didn't do or say, such as stealing the sweater she loaned me to wear when I was visiting. I had put it back in her drawer before I left. Even worse, she'd say something that belittled me as a human being. Or Daddy would tell me what I thought about something when that's not what I thought at all. Really? They hated their brothers – each of them had one – and were quite competitive with them. Same as mother was with her own mother. Was she competitive with her children, too? I think she was. She wanted no one to rise above her.

What I am starting to realize as I move through this journey of grief and loss – the loss of Trip, of never having parents who were present in a caring way, of never being truly seen by them, and the absence of love and self-love for so much of my life – that gradually a better opinion of me is developing, more compassion, more acceptance of my choices, my responses to my life. Now, I am beginning to like me. I can see what makes me *me*. Most days, at least. Can I forgive myself for my mistakes and lack of belief in myself? For my tendency to fail to speak up for me and my views, for holding grudges? I'm getting there. Or, hope that I am.

I think Trip, in his life and death, *has* been a catalyst for change in me. He is helping me to be a stand-up self. At least more of one.

Chapter Nine

"Know what's weird? Day by day, nothing seems to change. But pretty soon, everything's different."

~ Bill Watterson (from Trip's collection of quotes)

"I'm ambidextrous – I used to play with both hands in tennis and everything else, but now I mostly write with my left hand and throw things with my right."

25 Random Things About Me #15. Trip Lucas, Facebook.

I am still going over and over Trip and his life, my part in it, looking for clues. Where did I mess up? Where did I do something good for him? There's a journal entry from the one Trip that started on the day he left for school in France during his third year at UVA.

"Thur. Jan 14th. Nothing special. Woke up, finished packing, called [girlfriend]. I finished shopping w/ mom – bought a hairbrush, an International Driving Permit & map of Europe. 2:30, mom drove me to Dulles. She cried, I did too, a little."

I remember this exchange as we stood there waiting in line in Dulles:

"Trip, get out of this line. This is *my* dream."

"That's not why I'm doing it, mom."

That's what *he* thought. How do we know we're not trying to live a parent's unlived life? It happens often that a kid does try, thinking it is his own choice. I have been told that Carl Jung said "The best thing a parent can do for his child is to fully live his own life." If so, then the child won't feel compelled to live the parent's unlived life. Often, we see someone trying to do just that, but it doesn't suit them. Think of the men who become doctors or lawyers because that's what their fathers had wanted for themselves but had not done it. Sometimes, there are men whose fathers were in their chosen professions, but it did not resonate with the sons who tried to follow their fathers. Some of the sons have felt like failures because the job wasn't for them. As for me, I think that in the first part of my adult life, I lived a part of my mother's *lived* life – married to an alcoholic, co-dependent on him, unhappy. Then, my life gradually morphed into *my* life. I don't think my latter one is necessarily *her* unlived life, but it could be. It sure is better than the one she lived in. I am grateful for that.

I went to France to see Trip, to visit France for the first time, and to relish through him a piece of my own parent-squashed dream of majoring in French (I began college as a French major but switched because the class was so far ahead of me in readings), of attending a year of school in France and living in France for at least a year or so. After that, in my plan for my life, I would have been an interpreter at the UN. I viewed that as being a way of connecting cultures and people. Now I see that I have done that with clients by helping them to connect with their inner cultures, their own unknown.

Years later, I thought New York would have eaten me alive because I am such a country mouse. Maybe not, maybe I would have been worldly and strong in my own self after living abroad. Certainly, I was becoming a little bit more that way at that point in my life when Trip went to France for school.

It was during that time of attending school in Aix en Provence that one of Trip's entries in his diary is worth pondering and sad considering his suicide.

"My friend, C, committed suicide last weekend, 4/10/88, at his mom's house in D.C. I helped him learn English when he first arrived at St. Chris when I was in 8th grade; we always ate meals together when we were in Newcomb Hall [University of Virginia]. "Cela veut rien dire" – Camus? - I wonder."

"Why did C commit suicide? Why can't I comprehend this? I want to try to forget so that I don't do something similar. He never said anything mean, and he always smiled when he could. Maybe he didn't have a long-term goal. Mine has been to come to France and

be enlightened w/o becoming snotty. Now that I have discovered how to get along with both my French and my Italian, I need something more substantial.

In between being with Trip in Aix en Provence and going to visit my daughter Carter who was spending a year with a family in Norway, I spent a few days in Paris. I was hosted by the family of our former exchange student, Anne Violaine Bornen. They insisted on putting me up in a boutique hotel near their home in Versailles. Jean, Anne-Violaine's father, met me when I arrived from Marseilles at the Gare du Lyon. I enjoyed an evening of dinner with Anne-Violaine, her parents and her brother, François, at their home. I already knew François because he had spent the same summer in Virginia as Anne-Violaine but with another family. I will never ever forget him, either, because he told his host family that I was the "crème de la crème". How could I possibly forget such flattery or the person who said it?

The following day, Jean gave me a personally guided tour of some of his favorite sections of Paris and Versailles on my first full day. I could not have asked for more. The Champs Elyseé, Cathedrale de Montmartre, and more. He pointed out the amateur artists as we enjoyed a beer up top above the Cathedrale. He was one of those artists himself. Jean had done a painting of the little farmhouse in oil and gave it to me, signed by him. It's hanging in my home to this day. Our last stop was the Palace of Versailles, including la petit ferme of Marie Antoinette. His comments and enthusiasm as a local combined with his Franco-European understanding of the world, his own Sunday-painter talent, and his graciousness sprinkled with charm were the best. Near the end of the afternoon, I had a most unusual experience – think Twilight Zone or yet another experience of what Carl Jung would have described as coming from the collective unconscious and connected to other myths and cultures. Jean and I were standing on cobblestones at one end of the Champs Elyseé. My memories may be distorted or fuzzy over time, but this is how I remember it: in the middle was the lovely green median with mature plantings. Impressive, official-looking buildings were situated on either side. There was a low chain to keep foot traffic off this end that, as I remember it now, had a small fountain. Jean, who spoke no English, was telling me about the importance of this spot, but my ears, exhausted from listening to his non-stop French all day, were feeling infested with a thick fuzz. And my mind trying to respond in French, was tired. The rest of my body was tired, too. I felt as if blood was draining down my legs and out through my feet onto the cobblestones underneath. I understood little of what I was hearing, but I told myself I would look up this place in my guidebook as soon as I got back to my room. When I did, I discovered that we had been standing at the Place de la Concorde, on the very spot where the guillotine had stood during the French Revolution, where heads, including those of Marie Antoinette and Louis XVI, had rolled. And blood everywhere. I wrote a poem about that spot. The professor said that it was the best thing I'd written in that class. It was bloody, dramatic, and stormy/angry, the way he liked things.

Back at my lodging, feeling tired and a little homesick, I called home. Joe answered, sounding quite surprised to hear me on the phone, almost as if he had been caught with his hand in a cookie jar. He clearly had not been thinking of me. On my end, I felt nothing and heard nothing resembling the warmth of a caring voice. Nothing but the emptiness and the disconnect between us that was the truth of our relationship. Had I called because I had hoped it would be otherwise? Just as I often had when calling home to my parents back in the day? I was always disappointed but ever hopeful for something else. Joe was emotionally gone; I knew it, but I still held that small bit of hope for a different reality. All that happened at the very same time that various improvements and changes were being made at our house. There was little reason to make it better for our sake, but I had been stubborn about wanting to see my vision of it take shape. I was still going through familiar motions while the inner me was changing. There had never been much between Joe and me – except for a bushel of great kids - and I was finally accepting that and getting ready to stand on my own two feet. The kids were about to leave home, too. It occurs to me as I write that it is sad mother had never been able to do what I would soon. She was fierce, but not in a way that furthered her own growth.

After Paris, I visited Carter in Norway, and met the lovely, large (five children, one set of twins) and happy family who were welcoming and fun for her. It is interesting to me that both Carter and Trip were spending extended time in other countries in the same year. It didn't seem as if either one was influenced by the other's plans. They just happened at the same time. Both were enriched for having gone. It was gratifying to me because even though I hadn't been allowed such a time, at least the next generation made it. I think that that may be the way healing and growth happen through generations. Each plays an incremental part.

A year later, Trip, his sisters, Joe and I, and our parents assembled on a Saturday in May on the Lawn at the University of Virginia along with thousands of others to witness the Final Exercises for Trip's class in the College of Arts and Sciences. Each May, the graduating class of both undergraduate and graduate students process down the Lawn from the Rotunda toward Old Cabell Hall. It is an impressive scene, one to make any student and parent proud. Carter, who was about to enter college, was impressed. She said, "I want a piece of that." In Trip's year, each student was allowed six guests who could have seats in chairs placed on the Lawn. In Trip's case, that was his immediate family. His grandparents stood along the sides with the hundreds of others. That part of the exercise lasted about two hours. Soon after, Trip received his diploma, a handshake, and congratulations at the French House from the head of the French department. That time, Trip was clearly happy, different from the way he had looked at high school graduation.

Prior to graduation, Trip had turned down an invitation from the language department to stay there, be a Teaching Assistant, and earn his master's at the same time. He turned it down, saying that he was tired of school and just wanted to float for a while.

Settled back at home, Trip worked selling water treatment systems, hay baling, construction, and other odd jobs that turned up. One day during that time, he asked me what his father's income was. I made a tactical mistake when I answered him. I told him what – as far as I knew - because Joe didn't tell me much. For several years, he had proudly shown me the company statement that accompanied his commission each month. Then he stopped doing that. What Trip wanted to know was what it cost to have the life we had. I gave him a guesstimate. Joe's income was always changing, depending on the market, but for many years it had been very good. By the same token, for a lot of our marriage, he hid money info from me, especially the many times he was using our money for risky investments, ones – many of them - that did not turn out well.

Looking back, I am pretty sure that whatever Trip did, my guess, was the benchmark by which he measured himself. It's quite possible that he missed his own "mark", that his calling may have been to be a teacher. His comment about that was, "I don't want to live on a teacher's salary." He was happy enough just floating for a year and a half. I worried about him – when was he going to figure out where, when, and how to start his life - but happy having him at home.

When he said to me one day, "I like the life of a housewife", I began to think it was time to push that bird out of the nest. I told him that I wasn't invested in *what* he did, only that I thought it was time he got busy finding his own way. That's when Joe became highly invested in *what* Trip did and pushed him toward joining the military. Joe had wanted to be a career military himself, but he had not followed through. Perhaps he thought Trip was like him and needed the discipline and would like the military. Trip wasn't like his father. He had plenty of self-discipline; his dreams were his. His life was his, not his father's. Nevertheless, in deference to his father, and maybe out of curiosity, he interviewed with two branches of the military, the Army and the Navy. They pursued him because they were impressed with his language ability. He chose the Army. Before he left, he bought another used vehicle from a friend of his, a Jeep Cherokee with 200K miles on it.

I worried about him then, too, the same as I had when he went to UVA. I can see, looking back, that even as smart as he was, he did need guidance, someone to bounce thoughts and ideas with him. Someone to appreciate who he was as a person. I didn't feel qualified for the man entering the world of work score. I am sure he knew I cared, though. Throughout his life, he was lucky enough to have a few men who played that role. One who also cared was my maternal grandfather, Gigi, Trip's great-grandfather. When Trip was born, Gigi visited him when he was still in the hospital nursery and predicted that he was going to be a smart young man. He was right. When I spoke with Townley in the process of this writing, he, too commented on how smart Trip was. A few of his mentors were teachers. There was Townley, then one or two at UVA. His father-in-law before, during, and after his marriage to Kim was always helpful to Trip. Peter, the family friend, was one of those who cared about Trip. Then there was Pete, older than Trip, a seasoned rock-climber, musician, and man of many talents in Austin, who meant a lot to Trip. I think he did some mentoring, too, just by being a part of Trip's life.

After basic training, Trip was not allowed to pass Go but was sent straight to the Defense Language Institute in Monterey, California, to learn either Farsi or Chinese. He wasn't excited about either one, preferring any of the European languages.

Trip learned Mandarin well, and he also learned that he did not give a fig for the military. According to a Chinese grandmother at the Monterey Aquarium, he spoke the language well. She told me that as we stood next to each other in front of the huge aquarium. Years later, I was with him on a chair lift in Vail as he spoke Chinese to a Chinese woman. I was proud and happy, like only a mother can be.

"...I've spent more hours studying Mandarin than required for a full undergrad degree (before the Defense Language Institute gave degrees), yet I'm so rusty now that I doubt I could read a children's book." Excerpt from 25 Random Things About Me #6, Trip Lucas, Facebook.

He was still in Monterey when his college girlfriend, also from Richmond, Virginia, wanted to break up with him. He went AWOL one weekend to come home to try to talk her out of it. That's the first time he thought about suicide. The girlfriend called me to tell me that he was threatening to jump off a bridge.

Going AWOL caused him to lose his high-security clearance. Joe was furious. "You've disgraced yourself and ruined your time in the military," Joe said. I was secretly quite happy because I could see he was being groomed for the intelligence/spy game - he told me that his next assignment was probably going to be in a cave somewhere, listening to secret transmissions from state enemies - and I did not want to see him doing that, or getting involved in any of the intelligence aspects, for lots of reasons. Mainly, it was his sensitivity. I thought being in the spy world would have seriously affected his psyche and his personality, and he would become hardened and/or disillusioned.

What wound up happening was that the army sent Trip on a different track than Intelligence, a track that took him to Georgia and then to Ft. Hood, Texas, where he was when he was honorably discharged at the end of his obligation.

That year, I had taken one graduate class in the Spring session and was just about to begin my first full year. In Trip's pile of letters that he had kept, there is one from me written at about that time. I wrote about taking the first steps to a new career and how I felt about that. I left unspoken how much the rest of my life would also be changing. Even though I left that unspoken, I was aware that Trip could, and would, perceive that his father and I were going to divorce.

Life went on from there until now when Trip is gone. I am starting over again, trying to live my life, yet I am still not losing what must be my fantasy that if I can just figure out how to undo this horror I am living, I will get Trip back.

What I keep finding are the ways throughout my life that I let myself down. I let myself down when I didn't know any way other than to take mother's insults and intrusive verbal and physical abuses, some of that was in the too-personal and physical realm when I was a teenager. Those and my father's sexual moves and comments. All were shaming and inhibiting. I hid myself even more. It's hard to shake the memories of the times daddy said and did things to me that were sexually intrusive, abusive, and disrespectful. The evening in our living room is a gauzy memory I'd like to forget because remembering brings back the icky feeling. He was drinking, drunk. He kissed me with his tongue in my mouth when we were standing. Later, we were sitting on the sofa, and he tried to put his hand up my Bermuda shorts, saying, "No wonder the boys don't come around; they can't get their hands in your pants." I was 15 years old. Why didn't I scream, yell, bite, and kick like a horse fighting capture? Why? My father took something important from me that evening. It was an ineffable but essential piece of my being. I can still bring back that feeling and shiver or feel disgusted. When I went in the kitchen to tell mother what had just happened, she said, her speech laced with booze, while waving her hand in the air, "Oh, he shouldn't do tha-at."

That egregious behavior did not happen again, but Daddy's talking about my body never stopped. Before puberty, he called me and my friend Maude and the "Crisco Kids", as in fat in the can. After puberty, it was always about my breasts, how they changed size, if I was skinny or had given birth, or whatever occurred to him, sometimes based on what I was wearing. It makes my skin crawl to think of it. I used to say to myself when the women's movement had begun that I had felt that my body belonged to my father, or he thought it did, even long after I was married. He and mother enjoyed their sex life and liked to comment on others' sex life or just sex in general. Mother was enthralled with the genitalia of both genders. After Trip was born, mother said to me, "It was a lot easier going in than coming out, wasn't it?" I was/am grossed out by them both.

 Forward to five years after the living room experience when I was in college, but home for Spring break. A lifelong friend had one of his fraternity brothers in town and asked me to go with them and a few others for an evening of dancing at a local roadhouse. When he and the rest in the same car took me home, the visiting guy walked me to the door and kissed me goodnight. Daddy, well-oiled, was waiting at the door with an umbrella because it was raining. He tut-tutted about the kiss as I walked in, and the next morning, he took me to his office to lecture me about what good girls do and don't do, using an example of some girl who slept with one of his fraternity brothers in college. Really?

Why didn't I remind him what he had done to me five years before? Why? I was too submissive and not anywhere near outraged enough at the time. He was my father, and I was afraid of him. I remember thinking then that he was a dirty old man. So, am I thinking that if I had been stronger then, I would have been for Trip, too? For some reason, my mind is linking these things. They all have me beating up on myself. Placing blame on me. The "it's all your fault" accusation. I can see one thing very clearly now that I probably wasn't aware of for so many years. I did not want to object or argue – with my parents, with Joe, or with kids, either – if it would precipitate an argument. I was way too intimidated by the ones I had witnessed between my parents and would not speak up. I had no confidence that I could convince anyone of anything, either. I just kept my thoughts and opinions to myself and silently went my own way. No doubt, there are times when one *ought* to stand up for oneself. Out loud. I am *still* unlearning those unhelpful ways of self-preservation and learning, or trying to, ways of growth and becoming. I think it will take a few more years.

In the Ft. Hood area, Trip met Kim, who later became his wife. They began dating and continued to after he moved to Austin for graduate school. Along the way, he lost his shirt investing in rental housing near Ft. Hood because, at that very time, the Army had decided to shrink the size of Ft. Hood so much that the rental market deflated. Kim's father was instrumental in Trip's learning a lot about plumbing, carpentry, and whatever skills he needed to fix up his two rental houses.

He migrated from the Ft. Hood area to Austin to earn an international MBA in information management at the University of Texas. He wanted the international part because of his interest in living in foreign places.

Soon, he had a job with an international corporation based in New York. The company sent Trip to work in France. That was his Bre'r Rabbit in the Briar Patch moment, a reference to The Uncle Remus stories by Joel Chandler. Brer Rabbit kept saying to Brer Fox, "Please don't throw me in the briar patch!" because it was the very place where he knew he could elude the fox. Trip did software work there and loved being in France. When that ended, he was brought back to the States to find another position within the company, but it would be at New York headquarters until further notice. What he gained from that job was expertise in the current most desired software for businesses with big inventories. That made him attractive to a lot of corporations.

What attracted Trip at the time, along with the software world, was back in Austin, Texas: a special woman, Kim, and a lifestyle. He left the large corporation to go back to Austin, where, in no time, he found a job with a dot.com company. That was right up his alley. All the employees were just like him: high energy and high creativity. Like him, they had the same work habits. They would go full bore for days at a time and then kick back until the next spurt.

Trip had found out he liked Austin as well or better than most of the people who have spent any time there. He became one of the legions of walking ads for it with his "Keep Austin Weird" t-shirt. He enjoyed the weird past times and festivals, such as the annual O'Henry Pun-Off held every May.

"I love puns and 'corny' jokes. I used to go to the O'Henry Pun-Off every summer in Austin. One favorite Joke from my sister, Dana, is: "How many mice does it take to screw in a light bulb? Two, the trick is getting them in there." Another favorite is: A man walked out of the bar and got in his car and a policeman came over. "Sir, your eyes seem to be bloodshot. Have you been drinking?" "Officer, your eyes seem to be glazed. Have you been eating doughnuts?" #25,

25 Random Things About Me, Trip Lucas, Facebook

After Trip died, Kim called to offer condolences. She gave me her contact info so that I could get in touch later. Kim said, "We were uncertain and ambivalent about getting married, though we talked about it many times." Were they going to, or were they not? When they finally decided to do it, it was almost last minute, with no big amount of advance planning. They just went to Telluride and set it up once there. I had asked Trip if they would include any family or not. He hemmed and hawed. My answer came after the fact: they did not invite anyone else.

I have the postcard Trip sent to me of Bridal Veil Falls in Telluride saying,

"Hey mom, we got married here." That was all I had until later when I saw some photos taken at the scene. His writing had obscured the date stamp.

My visit to Trip and Kim at their Barton Springs home in Austin was fun and interesting on a lot of levels. I had been to visit earlier when I was just out of grad school and Trip was still working on his grad degree. He was living in small grad school digs and Kim was there visiting, but the Barton Springs place was larger and in a beautiful area of town. There were good areas for my daily runs, and then the Springs themselves, with their refreshing and shockingly cold water for swimming or just cooling off. Riding bikes around town with Trip and Kim was almost out of fiction or a movie: music on every corner, the legendary bats flying out from under the bridge in the evening, and on one ride, finally winding up on the Capitol steps. I felt as if Chariots of Fire music should have been playing.

It was there at the Barton Springs home that I got my first real understanding of Trip's touch with the décor. Some of this had been evident in his grad school place: the bookshelves he built using the Skandia system's hardware that was completely able to be dis-assembled and re-assembled. All quite architectural. But here, in the combination galley kitchen/dining area/living room there was a comfortable and cushy light green sofa. On one wall, he had spray-painted a shadow of a bicycle. It was clever in a subtle way. On another wall, Trip had built an intricate climbing gym with carpeted spaced-apart steps for the two kitties they had adopted. It went from floor to ceiling and was on the wall facing the sofa. On the end, where the glass doors led to the enclosed patio, I think there was a dining table and another chair or two.

In a few years hence when Trip was with Laura, they took me to the O'Henry Pun-Off. Part funny/weird, part fun. And hot. Very hot.

We sat in the backyard of the O'Henry Museum in downtown Austin, sweltering in the Texas heat. All the audience were outside, sitting on the ground, and most were not shaded by the one tall spreading tree. The sound system was just barely helpful that day, but I heard a few groans. Trip loved it – the nerdiness, the wordplay, the whole thing.

Trip is a loss I will never get over. The fact that he's gone is what I am slowly getting used to, though I notice that I've started to sometimes call my dog Trip. She doesn't look a thing like him, but she's smart and sweet and sensitive. Reminiscent of Trip.

Chapter Ten

"An optimist may see a light where there is none, but why must the pessimist always run to blow it out?"

~ Michel de Saint-Pierre (Trip's quote collection)

Many may remember that the bottom fell out of the dot.com boom in a relatively short time. People like Trip, still paying off their grad school loans and just getting started, needed work, and it wasn't readily available, especially in Austin. He had experience in the tech world, but that world is overcrowded in Austin. His dot.com job ended. He took anything he could get. He took a part-time job as a schoolteacher for grade school kids who had a variety of disabilities, most of them learning ones. I've been told he was good at it, and he said he liked it. I had thought for years that he would be a great teacher, but he had that benchmark in his mind and would tell me, "I don't want to live on a teacher's salary." His other part-time job was doing wildlife removal. For that, he removed bees from attics and walls, rescued/removed deer caught in weird places or hit on the highway, snakes, mice, cats, wildcats (er, maybe), you name it. His farm-country upbringing groomed him for many of the skills needed in that job. He liked that, too, but wanted more income.

When software jobs started to be available again, there was a kicker: a large proportion of them had become short-term, six-month contract positions. The contracts had been bought up by Larry Ellison of Oracle and, later, another company named Calypso. There were no benefits involved with the contracts. That saved corporations the expense and hassle of full-time employees. It meant as Trip said about his generation, "We are screwed." No gold watch, no retirement, no health insurance, and no job security, not to mention constant moving. Continuing education, a necessary part of the rapidly changing tech environment, was not provided, either. He really was screwed, but he wouldn't give up. The worst thing about that setup is that whoever bought the contract *owned* the employee. After the six months were up, or the job ended, he or she was out on the cyber pavement looking for another job. These were people with graduate degrees.

As Trip's work life changed and deteriorated, he got sick – bronchitis. He and Kim were struggling to get along with each other and then, they decided to part. That sent him into a place he didn't think he could survive. He thought of killing himself then. It feels awful to me to think of talented, smart Trip feeling so unable to appreciate his own worth. And his looks. "He's so handsome", said my friend Betsy – over and over; she would say it whenever she saw him. Thanks to the intervention of our family friend, Peter, who thought the world of Trip, he came to live with me until he could get back on his feet. It took a while. That was the time he stayed with me for nine months. At the end of that time, he first moved to Florida for a potential job, took a couple of short-term ones, got a job in Atlanta, and was there for a year or so. While there, he worked for another international corporation doing software and began dating a woman who not only worked for the same corporation but was his superior. It was verboten in that company to date a co-worker. That was an "oops" that Trip knew might get him. It did. Someone figured it out when Trip and the woman each said separately that they had gone to Vail over Christmas vacation. It was like Trip to take a chance on something that he thought was a ridiculous requirement. He wasn't a troublemaker and was always a law-abiding person, but he had his principles, and they cost him that job. Maybe that kind of thing just runs in the family. My maternal grandparents met and fell in love when he, seven years older, was her Latin teacher and Basketball coach in her high school. He had taken the job to earn money for law school, which was where he was headed next. They dated, and years later, here I am, a product of that rule-breaking couple.

As I write and think about Trip's life, I see so many times I might have asked him the right questions. The ones that would have come from an adult in his life who felt more secure in herself, who had wrestled with her own choices a bit more, who had thought she *had* choices. I think I was inadequate for the task of being Trip's parent – or maybe anyone's for that matter. I loved him and his sisters, for sure, and he knew that, but maybe it wasn't enough. It seemed to me that he kept struggling to do work that would give him value in his father's eyes. Or maybe it was just in the culture's value system – lots of money and the power it brought. Was it really where his heart was? That's what I could have asked him. If I had read the quote from a 2012 George Lucas interview with Oprah, I would have brought that up with Trip. Heck, I wish there had been a George Lucas who said it when I was young. It's excellent advice.

"Don't listen to your peers, don't listen to the authority figures in your life—your parents— and don't listen to the culture. Only listen to yourself. That's where you're going to find the truth." ~ George Lucas

Trip had an intensity about him that wouldn't let up on his expectations for himself. My Jungian astrologer/friend looked at Trip's chart soon after his death. She told me that she was sure she had seen the chart before, but I knew she hadn't. Then she realized that the one she was remembering was that of Robin Williams, the actor. She had viewed his chart when he took his life, which was just a month or so before Trip. She told me that he and Trip were born on the same day but 15 years apart and that Robin's chart showed the same intensity. It may well be the same trait that Kim's dad noted about Trip wanting to learn something and then just doing it. He was driven in a way, but I'm not sure that's what everyone would notice about him.

"Surfing and life. I'm just starting to learn surfing. There's a lot to it – and nothing to it. Once you figure out the timing and learn to read the waves, the actual surfing part seems to be pretty easy so far. Of course, I've got a lot to learn. The biggest lesson I had from the first day was that it will exhaust you if you try to catch every wave. So much of surfing is learning how to read the waves and learning timing so that you don't waste your energy on the bad ones. You have to let some seemingly good waves go by. Others you might not be able to tell until you're on them. You waste some energy, and you let them pass. I'm not much for waiting, but in surfing, you're burning yourself out if you don't learn to wait. That seems a lot like the opportunities in life. If you're busy paddling after the wrong wave, then you'll miss the right one that you can't see coming behind it. This applies to relationships as well." ~ Trip Lucas, Facebook

There's a description of surfing in a book, Kook, written by Peter Heller, a good and successful author. What Trip wrote is so similar that I had to look up when Kook was published. I was wondering had Trip consciously or unconsciously echoed what Peter Heller wrote. Trip's collection of quotes, thoughts, and Random Things appeared on Facebook in early 2009. Kook was published in 2010, so I don't think Trip had read it. And I don't think Trip would fail to give credit to the author of those words if they were someone else's. I think I know *that* much about my son. It does surprise me that Trip had learned to surf, but then I could easily not have known. I didn't know that Trip had skied Telluride at least a couple of decades before I moved to Colorado. Trip told me when he was skiing with me after I moved here.

Trip was often trying to figure out relationships. I get it. It is hard to know what you want, how to do it and, again, which is the *right* one. When you are a good-looking guy, as Trip was, it must have been harder. Women flocked to him. He had a presence about him, a presence to others and to the world around him.

Also true was that Trip had yet to meet The One, and he knew that but held out hope. He couldn't stay out of the water where they were all swimming. How would he meet her if he was on the shore and she was in the water?

My terrible guilt in Trip's relationship department has to do with his father's and my relationship. There's no way we showed him a positive picture. I was extremely averse to arguing because of had witnessed the brawls between my parents. They were frightening and painful to witness. I was inhibited by that, which resulted in my not wanting to question Joe about anything. Once, when he hid a purchase from me, I discovered the receipt. It was for a Jon boat, motor, and trailer for duck hunting. That time, I did question why he hid it from me; he said, "Because I didn't want you to want to spend the same amount on yourself." *That* should have been *worth* an argument. I can imagine now what I might have said then what I would say now. I will say one thing about Joe: he never denied it when he did or said something akin to chopping down the apple tree.

His father had noticed that about him, too. He owned up to mistakes and missteps. And seemed to do so without shame.

That voice in my head spoke to me two or three years after my life-changing stop-light experience. I was shuffling through a church parking lot, feeling so out of place within myself and my marriage. It said, "You *can* get a divorce." I didn't ask it "how" or where to start. It took me another 11 years.

I did what I had done with my parents: I kept to myself. I *did* trust myself, but I did not speak up about it. I just guarded myself against any storm, especially ones that might arouse an argument. I could not handle anything, even close to a fight.

Finally, I sought out clergy, hoping for support or encouragement, saying I thought that Joe was dependent on alcohol and that it was a problem. The two men of the cloth doubted me. "They are coming to dinner at our house. I will pay attention," the elder one said. Of course, he didn't corroborate my say-so. Neither of them gave me support or understanding. They were patriarchs, even though they would vehemently deny that label.

I often felt that way around my parents. What language *was* I speaking that they so often acted as if they didn't hear me, let alone understand me. Or they acted as if I wasn't even in the room. They would make decisions about where I was going to school or camp, or what I would wear to cotillion, or to a special dance during junior year in high school. That was the worst – a white organdy puff-sleeved dress with a baby blue sash? Really? I was almost 17, not 7. I was embarrassed when I had to wear that dress. None of my friends dressed that way.

But if I could see that Trip had yet to figure out the world of his work, why did I just sit back and watch him struggle without trying to engage him in a real discussion of what he wanted? I had no idea how to encourage him in that department or what to say. He did have many choices and time on his side. With him, I had little wisdom. Or I wasn't confident enough to access what I did have. What he needed was a mentor. One who understood his talents and his unique process. One who wasn't afraid to speak up.

There's also the possibility that I was almost as much in the dark as he, just at a different place in life. Same ole me –little confidence, a scooch of know-how and experience regarding my own work, but that was about it. Everything else was new, including my location.

Once again in Austin, after his time in another state with the corporation that fired him for dating his colleague, Trip re-connected with his many friends. One of the friends he ran into was Laura. I think he had known her before, but they had each been married then. By this time, they were both divorced. She had three daughters in school, one in college, and two of them were living in the house with their father, who was nearby. The youngest daughter, still in middle school, spent weekends at Laura's. Laura and Trip became an item. Then they moved in together. He looked for work in the software world, worked out at the gym, did yoga, and went climbing.

I visited Trip and Laura when they were settled in the first place they had together. They had been together for five years when Trip took his life. The first place was very small and not such a nice neighborhood, but inside, Trip had done his usual magic with the décor. Once, Trip said to me, "Mom, you can make a room look good, but not always comfortable".

As I see it, comfort for him meant a cushy green sofa along with his self-made art on the wall. There was a green sofa everywhere he lived. Was it the same sofa? Not sure. And were there any real seating areas with perhaps a chair near the sofa? Maybe not in each house. Not sure.

In this place, as in all his, it was comfortable and had an artsy look that included a bit of whimsy. The art on one wall was made up of 33 album covers – the Rolling Stones and more – artfully arranged. There were real bicycles on the floor to one side of the albums. They added to the look. That, bookshelves, and the audio-video set-up were all in the small living room.

It was in that house where Trip showed me how he fixed his yummy salmon burgers from Costco. They come frozen. He rubbed the frozen burger with agave syrup and seafood seasoning and, after cooking in a hot skillet, inserted it into a bun with catsup and sliced tomato. Add a salad or veggie, and voilà, dinner. I still make those burgers. And think of Trip.

Life with Laura introduced Trip to her three daughters. There were always females around Trip. Trip's four sisters, Kim's one daughter, now Laura's three daughters. Psychologists might say it meant Trip had to develop his feminine side, but I don't know if that was true of Trip. He was a sensitive guy. I think that part of him was well-developed but still might have needed some growth or some particular wisdom.

One of Trip's 6-month contract jobs after moving in with Laura was in Memphis. He liked his co-workers and the job, pretty much the same as usual, but in that case, he had trouble with the energy of Memphis. Something about it bothered him. I think it might have been the residue of racism. And there was the commute. Trip and Laura took turns commuting. First, Laura went to Memphis one weekend, then Trip to Austin the next. It was grueling, and near the end of the contract, Trip's boss and he agreed that he wasn't happy there. The boss would have liked to keep Trip after the contract period, but it would not have been the best situation. Again, Trip was disappointed, even a bit depressed, and told me how he felt, but I thought he had worked through it.

The summers that Trip and Laura came to visit me, we hiked and played some tennis. Trip and I tried to get Laura to play tennis, but she didn't feel that she could keep up with us, so she took pictures of Trip and me on the court. I am grateful to have those now. Trip took countless photos of wildflowers on one of those hikes. There are so many I had to put my copies on a separate drive. We went to a couple of the free concerts in Vail, too. The two of them seemed happy together, but work for Trip was a constant issue.

It was a year or more after that wildflower visit that Trip landed the software job with an international company at its office in Slough, a town just outside London.

As in all his jobs, Trip liked his co-workers and his boss. The boss liked him and wanted to find him a full-time position within that company – he would have gone to the office in Germany and was excited about the possibility - but the headhunter who had brokered this position wanted too much money for Trip. He was once again disappointed.

Before they left Europe, Trip took Laura to his favorite French locales, including Calanque d'en Vau. That is the place he took me when I had been there visiting him. It is a small, world class spot on the Mediterranean and where I want to deposit the rest of Trip's ashes. I know he would like that.

During one of their visits to me, Trip told me that he and Laura were thinking about having a baby. We were standing in my living room on another Colorado blue sky day. I was taken by surprise and delight. Laura was three years older than Trip. She was 47 at the time. She had 3 daughters already. Two were well on their way, with one not quite in high school. I replied that I knew he'd be a great dad, and I had always hoped he would have children, but Laura was 47. I told him I was not sure I would have wanted to start over at that stage. But I could see that they both liked the idea – and I must admit, it was exciting for me to contemplate. I feel sure that if Trip had been a father, he would not have taken his life.

Chapter Eleven

"Every gun that is made, every warship launched, every rocket fired, represents, in the final analysis, a theft from those who hunger and are not fed, who are cold and are not clothed. This world in arms is not spending money alone. It is spending the sweat of its laborers, the genius of its scientists, the hopes of its children." - Dwight D. Eisenhower, in Trip's quote collection.

It was summer, almost seven years after Trip's death. I was feeling emotions in a way I had never felt them. I had always been sensitive to other's emotions as well as my own, but I had never been as easily moved to tears as I was at that time. I thought of Trip on his birthday on July 21st and cried. I thought of the fact that I was not getting any younger and teared up. I was still quite active and in good health, but that was no guarantee I would always be so. I remember good things and nice things and am grateful. And shed more tears. All kinds of stories – good, bad, sad, happy – moved me to tears.

Daily, on waking, I would get a cup of tea and begin to journal. Once that was finished and another cup of tea or two later – I sat in meditation. Letting the tears fall was what I did in my sanctuary house. At that time, it was a post-divorce healing that enabled me to begin the next phase of my life. It helped immensely. Then, I was doing that again. I was allowing, accepting, and feeling my way into wholeness once more. It was a healthy process. I hope that it would be healing again.

This time, the loss of Trip was the catalyst. Post-divorce, the grief was more over not having had a happy marriage and how that affected our kids. Added to that having to support myself and find my way in the world of work and life all over again. This time, my relationship with my son was something I remembered with immense gratitude along with the grief. I was not sorry that I took the long view in that I chose to have the child who turned out to be Trip. I chose to try to make a life with his father. I chose motherhood. Did I know what I was doing? No, but I trusted myself.

The losses and agonies of shame past that woke me in the middle of my nights were ones that had been with me for most of my life. The mega bomb loss of my son had re-opened them all. It was as if my unconscious was saying to me, "No way you are getting off without re-visiting these nagging and important burrs under your psychic saddle."

Here's one: "What about your parents? You think you can just whine about them and be free of that conundrum? The ones who didn't love their children. The ways they did not respect your body, or you as a person? Do you think that is just going to go away by itself?"

"Well, no, I guess not," I said, but not with lots of excitement about revisiting it. I didn't want to feel it anymore. In spite of myself, though, I did feel it when something reminded me. And then, tsunamis of memories kept flooding my consciousness through dreams or through my waking up in the morning.

In the healing process, it is one thing to remember but another to allow yourself to feel, in your body, the fear or trauma that keep you from being true to yourself at the time. A lot of psychotherapeutic wisdom, or belief, has it that for the bad moments in your life or the bad memories to heal, you must allow yourself to feel the feelings that you may well have shoved under your emotional rug because of the potential pain, the pain you were afraid to feel at the time. When you do, it usually brings tears, sadness, terrible body aches, and more that were not fully accepted at the time it all came down.

For me, after Trip's death, I buried myself in the business of the life celebrations of Trip. I felt shame and pain and did not, could not, wear them on my sleeve. I didn't want to share my shame or pain. It was too embarrassing. The perfect example is that dream I have already mentioned, the one in which I am lying in bed with a man who is naked. I am fully dressed and saying, "If I had known you would be naked, I would have gotten naked, too." The point is: I was not naked because I did not want to be completely seen, meaning in my psychological pain in the case of just about all the awful things that have happened in my life: my parents, my marriage when my favorite animals were hurt when anything hurt me. I was ashamed and did not want to be seen. Especially hanging out any of my dirty laundry.

How I dealt with my shame for years was to just keep myself to myself. When something happened that embarrassed or shamed me, I kept it in, even if it meant enduring more and more of the same. I could not, would not, tell my parents anything about me that wasn't forced out of me, or sometimes, even if they tried, I just did not speak up. It was a combo of being unknown and unseen and not wanting to be found out.

There was a book mother used to have that I noticed around the time I was 12. I had forgotten the exact title, but it was something like Children Are People Too. It looked like a textbook, and if I am right about the title, it makes me think that it was perhaps the beginning of a movement away from the authoritarian, reward-or-punishment, do as I say, not as I do, a shame-inducing way which was my parent's style of parenting. They appeared to think little about the idea that we might already have within us what we needed to become successful people and adults. That's my belief and that of many others as I am writing this.

I was curious about what mother read and thought. What I gathered from perusing the book was that it was written by a woman (pretty sure it was a woman) who postulated that many of her readers thought children were miniature uncivilized wild animals. That they needed to be kept in cages until a certain age. And told, over and over, how to behave. Whatever it was that I read didn't change my feelings toward and about my parents. Nor did it help alleviate the wounds that they inflicted on me and my sisters regularly.

I came to the conclusion that we were mother's experiment in Early Childhood Development – which was the name of a class she took in her Junior College, the school she left (I think she flunked out) after a year. The class taught her that the way to get a child to behave was to shame him or her. She was intrusive and shaming. *Proper Behavior* was her goal. She and Daddy were elitists, and the noblesse oblige sort of racists. Proper was according to Emily Post, of etiquette fame. To Mother, Emily Post was *the* guru one should heed. And then there was Dr. Basman, the pediatrician. His was the word of God, according to Mother.

Mother was intrusive in many ways, but one of the biggest occurred the year I was almost 16 when she told me that Dr. Basman (I still went to him for at least another year) said I should weigh 108 pounds, which was 5 less than my 113. A few months after that, I dieted until I weighed 108 and stopped menstruating. Without further ado, mother announced that she was taking me to Dr. Edmonds, a gynecologist, because I had stopped menstruating. She took me and then sat at the business end, watching while he put me in the stirrups and examined me. For what? Some terrible disease of the pelvis? If it was pregnancy she suspected, there would have been a new star in the east if that was the case. I still feel close to matricidal toward her over that. Did I say I can hold a grudge? For that and for telling me that Dr. Basman said I should weigh 108. I think she lied, that it was what *she* wanted me to think so that I would be thinner, always thinner than I was. I never did believe Dr. Basman said it. I just did not fit her ideal woman.

On top of both of those acts, she talked Dr. Edmonds into admitting me to the hospital for a glucose tolerance test to make sure I didn't have diabetes. One of my father's aunts had what I suspect was likely type II diabetes, and mother was certain that one of us would get it, too. I tried to get out of there by calling the doctor from the hospital bed, but mother had some sort of hold on him – or they had a little something going on between them that had nothing to do with my health. I've always had a question in my mind about that. She was quite the flirt – one of the many things that could start an argument with Daddy.

Thirty-plus years later, she tried to apologize to me. I was still ashamed and angry and wouldn't let her get beyond saying that she shouldn't have done that, should she? An apology would not have made *me* feel any better. I didn't care if she needed to ease her belatedly discovered conscience. And I wasn't big enough to let her do it or to spell out so many other things that had been just as wrong and hurtful. She had driven over from West Virginia, saying that she wanted to take me shopping. Shopping? We *never* went shopping together. If I needed something, she'd drop me off at one of the department stores in town and send me in, even for my first bra. Gads, I was glad. I sure didn't want Mother there commenting on my blossoming bosoms. If it was something like the party dress, she would have picked it out ahead of time. Forget how I liked it or even how it looked on me. Once I went to college, I was on my own. My $20 per month allowance had to cover everything. Wedding dress? Arranged and chosen by Mother, of course. I can't even go there.

I was suspicious of the shopping trip from the beginning. And I sure as heck did not want to go try on clothes in front of her and feel humiliated by her comments about my looks or size – ones like "Your lips are too fat." Or "Your feet are *so* flat!" Or the killer, "You should weigh 108." I was about to go to grad school and wanted a computer and a printer. Not clothes. I wound up selling my good 5-horse truck to pay for grad school.

Often, but especially after I had my therapy practice up and running and was working full time, Mother would say things like, "Aren't you coming home for your father's birthday?" As if, for one thing, I had nothing else to do, and as if, for the second thing, that *my* birthday didn't matter. She had arranged to have me born on my father's birthday since she was overdue, and the doctor had asked her if she had a preference. On top of that, she'd say to me every birthday of my life until she was almost dead, "Wasn't I smart to have you born on your father's birthday?". The whole idea makes me want to throw up.

Another thing was how she played favorites with my kids on the one occasion when they were all at her house without me. She rewarded one daughter (Antoinette) for being good and banished another one (Kate) to Nana's house because she was sitting under the piano saying, "I want my mommy." That must have pricked Mother's ego. My sisters and I have noted that Mother much preferred the grandsons to the granddaughters. There were only three grandsons. The other six were female. A mirror of the culture? White male supremacy, the Patriarchy.

Then there's my marriage. I told myself when things evolved the way they did – my being pregnant - that you could make a life with anyone. I found out not so much. Some people just don't meet you where you are, or maybe vice versa. Some suck you dry. Some are all about them.

I felt discounted in that relationship. Joe never had the protective, "I want to take care of you" intention or love within him. Or any curiosity about me or how I felt. We did not have the same approach to life and had few discussions about how to approach anything. He made unilateral decisions about purchases like a microwave, color TV, and cars for me. I felt discounted, but seldom did I speak up. I knew for sure, after we had the first set of twins that it wasn't going to last. He wasn't there for me but went on living his own life with us, his family, on the side. The thing that always got me was that I could not see my way to being able to go it alone with five kids. I didn't have the earning power and I really wanted to be fully present for the kids as they were growing up. He hadn't been interested or curious about any of our kids at birth or in babyhood. Almost acted as if they weren't his. With the last two, he didn't come to see them, or me, in the hospital until five days after they were born. Once they could walk and talk, then he started to notice. It's harder unless there are two of you sharing the responsibility. The other thing that gets me is that now I know I had personal power even then, but then I had no idea that I did. I also know I had some intelligence, energy, and creativity, but I didn't believe in myself back then. I believed what my parents told me.

Looking back, I am now able to recognize and appreciate the times in my two graduate programs when the faculty respected me and my work and my ideas. The School of Social Work that I attended offered a combined master's degree with the local Presbyterian Seminary through its School of Christian Education. Burned out and dogmatized by Catholicism, the last thing I wanted was to be a Christian educator, but I was interested in two things: theology, to try to figure out what I believed (nothing orthodox), and a course on art in the Bible/Old Testament because of all the literary references that are made to it. As a Catholic, you don't read the Bible. Instead, you hear pieces of it in sermons, more from the New Testament than the Old Testament. I had heard very good reports about the course on Art and the Bible. I got two master's degrees, one an MA in Christian Ed, and the other an MSW, Master of Social Work, which concentrated on the clinical knowledge and application that prepared me to be a therapist. In both cases, I was rewarded for my thoughts, abilities, and scholarship. And there were worthwhile mentors in the halls of those educational institutions. People who saw *me*.

If I have any roots or wings, they came from my loving maternal grandparents and my higher education. Other roots and wings come from the natural world and the animals I have always loved. I think my paternal grandparents were good people, but they had both died by the time I was 8. My first cousins were much closer to them because they lived right across the street from them. I was a tad intimidated by that grandfather – he seemed like an overwhelming personality, but to this day, I appreciate his foresight, his enjoyment of life, and what he stands for in my memory.

As for my Trip thoughts and tears, I think about him daily, who he was, his sensitivity, intelligence and talents, his hopes and dreams, the fun he had in his life and that I had with him, how much I miss him and wish he were here. I'm sad about his loss and the fact that he felt compelled to take his own life. I say I am used to his being gone by now. In some ways, I am. In others, not so much.

What gets me is how awful he must have felt on that last day. Why didn't I realize how bad it was? Was I just too afraid to face up to it? Again? My "old friend" Fear? - tribute to Simon & Garfunkel's Sounds of Silence, "Hello darkness, my old friend, I've come to talk with you again."

When I was in grad school to become a therapist, one of the requirements for us Master of Social Work students was to take a class on research. Worthwhile research involves a huge amount of replication of the same thing. It also requires good design and a trillion other details for it to be any good. I was not inclined to pursue that aspect of working in the mental health field. Someone has to do it, just not me.

In spite of my aversion to doing research, I have spoken with many parents who have lost children or family members to suicide and many who know a friend or family member who has experienced the same loss. Over and over, I hear, "he/she wasn't sleeping." It was true for Trip, too. Laura told me so. She said he hadn't been sleeping but was, instead, for at least the few weeks before he took his life, sitting in front of his computer, almost blankly staring at the screen.

I am inclined to talk *someone* into researching the lack of sleep aspect of suicide. It is a facet of depression. I think it might be quite significant in suicidal ideation. What to do about it if it is? I can't get Trip back, but maybe there would be an advocate for others or their loved ones dealing with depression. I don't believe that mental/emotional health is just in the brain. It is in the whole being, the body, and however else you want to look at a person. Once someone is already in a depression, they don't have much desire to get better or believe that it's possible. That's the trick: helping a person believe it is possible to get better.

During this period, I re-read Elisabeth Kubler-Ross's *On Death and Dying,* her first book and the one in which she named the five stages, and then I skimmed Elisabeth Kubler Ross & David Kessler's book *On Grief and Grieving.* It was written near the end of her life. The last part was written as she was slowly, but clearly, dying. In it, Kubler Ross wrote a whole chapter on her own grief as her life was nearing its end. It is enlightening for both those near death and for those who have lost a loved one.

The state of the planet and the changes that have occurred in my lifetime to the natural world, wild animal species and plants, and our climate add to my daily tears. The natural world is dear to my heart, and to see how the current culture has become so attached to profit, to "success", to money itself makes me extremely sad. Climate change hasn't just happened as a naturally occurring cycle. People have invited it since, at least the Industrial Revolution, when mankind began digging up natural resources and using them to pollute the air, water, earth, and the people on it. The "revolution" of chemicals that pollute, addict, and kill off species, including humanity, is another license almighty man has used for profit and death. I mourn the growing loss of the green world, and wildlife, the delicate balance. Rachel Carson's Silent Spring caused a mini awakening, but now, instead of people allowing themselves to be awakened, many are refuting what is right before their eyes. Lying to themselves and others. Come on, people. We aren't *that* stupid. What happened to living an ethical life? To be ethical? Corruption is rampant in business and in government. The Golden Rule is no longer "do unto others what you would have them do unto you." It is "the man with the gold makes the rules." Forget "we're all in this together." It's "every man for himself." This ship is sinking. Rapidly. Be glad if you have no grandkids. They won't suffer the consequences we have helped to create.

Trip saw what was happening to the planet and to do his part, he and Laura investigated becoming owners of a company that provided solar on rooftops. For whatever reason, perhaps the investment required to get started, they did not make it happen.

Chapter Twelve

"I rarely follow convention."

Trip Lucas, 25 Random Things About Me #26, Facebook.

In April of 2014, the year Trip died in September, I took a course called Opening to the Infinite. I was intrigued by the title and at that place in my life when I was asking myself what my purpose would be for the last third of my life. The course promised it would teach us to do remote viewing and to view our futures. The future viewing is what hooked me. I wanted to know my purpose in the last third of my life and if, by some slim chance, being the ever-hopeful romantic that I am, I might finally meet "The One", the love of my life, what I called "the man I love who loves me back."

The course creator and teacher, Stephan Schwartz, had been the leader of a group of Cold War remote viewers for the US Government. The course I attended may have been the prototype for what is now available online. I went in person to Esalen, the retreat center in California. What I "saw" in my future was a man whose face I could not see, though I somehow knew that I was drawn to him and that he was special to me. He was being tightly embraced from either side by Nana and Gigi, my two maternal grandparents who had been deceased for over twenty years. I was confused. Was this the man I had hoped for, and did I have to die to meet him? Was I going to die soon? I loved and was loved by those grandparents, so if they were embracing this man, it must mean something.

Stephan had suggested that we have someone present to record our viewings, even though he had taught us how to do the viewings. I was back home, impatient as I often can be, and shy about revealing to anyone else this part of me that might be seen as kooky, so I did not ask anyone, nor did I discuss my viewing with another person, even my analyst, at the time. I stayed puzzled about this until a month or so after Trip died when I realized that the man was Trip. He was my grandparents' first great-grandchild. They loved him and Gigi had announced after his first visit to see Trip in the hospital that he was "going to be a smart man."

*My great-grandparents lived well into my twenties, and it was great
to know them.*

25 Random Things About Me # 4. Trip Lucas, Facebook.

A few years later, I had a chance to speak with Stephan about the
viewing, asking him if I could have intervened in Trip's suicide had
I realized what it meant. He does think that some futures can be
altered if the timing is right. We didn't have time then to discuss
Trip's circumstances at any length or come to any conclusions.

I have recently read in an account by another Cold War viewer that
he believes everyone has the ability to do remote viewing. I agree
with that, but it is not something we all learned in kindergarten. It
was an awesome thing to have done, but it did not assuage my grief
or guilt. I am getting used to Trip being on "the other side" and think
more than ever that the veil is thin.

Recently, I had a synchronistic moment. I had been thinking about
Trip and came across an interview with Bruce Springsteen in the
AARP magazine about aging in general and about a new album that
deals with the "mysteries of life and death". He thinks that death is
not the end because when someone dies,

"You do lose their physical presence, but their physical presence is
not all of them, and it never was all of them, even when they were
alive. Spirit is very strong. Emotion is very strong. Their energy is
very strong, and a lot of this, particularly for people who are very
powerful, really carries after death."

It has been my experience as well. I haven't lost all of Trip. He
appears in dreams, and I have felt his presence, his spirit or energy
at times. In one dream he was hiding in a little place in the hallway
of my house in the dream. He surprised me by popping out when I
walked into the hall. Thoughts and images of him appear frequently,
sometimes words that I think have come from him.

Writing is a pursuit and passion that I might not have allowed myself
without the therapist who gave me a shove to get me off the horse
in my dream, along with the other moments and unexpected events

that have brought me to it. Then, there is the main catalyst, Trip. It's about time I began what has been a life-long passion and intense desire. Trip's birth and death have pushed me to do so.

I am grateful for the many other writers who have inspired me with their words – either on the page or in person. It is a tribe whose coattails I am holding on to with all my might. Now, a few years later, having listened to myself – and others – and started to write, and being involved in the process almost daily, I have had more moments, more gifts from within – or beyond. Maybe within and beyond are the same thing? So much richness seems to have come to me since Trip died. It isn't that my life didn't have richness and joy before, but it feels as if there is a different, deeper kind now, a kind of fullness, along with the loss and heartache. It's possible that I am more grateful for the "love that holds it all together" and more aware of its presence.

I have also been sustained and felt loved in a way by my dreams and some of the dream figures who have become spirit guides. It was Carl Jung who used something called "active imagination" with figures in his dreams. He had one or two who became guides for him.

Once, I had a dream in which Tyche, the horse love of my life, appeared to me at the edge of a wooded trail. She said, "I was your mother before you were born." She was a beautiful, talented, thoroughbred mare. I bought her through a dealer, so I did not know until later that she had been born and raised on a friend's farm in another town in Virginia. I often called her "little mother" and would have loved to have bred her, but we didn't have the facility or the know-how for that. I knew she would be a great broodmare, though, says one broodmare (me) about a potential other one. Imagine if she had been my mother in some way. How different I would be, but she did contribute to my experience of love. Perhaps because of her I am different than I might have been given the parents I had. The communication Tyche and I had was the best. We understood each other without human language but with one of trust. I am always grateful to her for being in my life.

By the way, he did appear, the one I had hoped for, the one I called "the man I love who loves me back." He did appear, not in the remote viewing, but later, he came into my life. I thought he was the love of my life. We had what he said was great chemistry, and I had the pleasure of experiencing the Irving Berlin song type of being in love. The one in which the singer hears "singing when there's no one there" and smells "blossoms when the trees are bare" and "All day long I seem to walk on air". I did that and kept tossing in my sleep at night, too. It was magical. It's the kind of love you don't have to think about or decide anything because it just *is*. But as it turns out, he did not feel the same way. That hurt. I had been used to those in my life who were all about them and who didn't love me. Those were deep and longstanding painful experiences. This was similar but different because I let myself start to believe that this relationship would be the antidote to the belief that I was unlovable, the belief that was inculcated by my parents and reinforced by my husband.

Never giving up on me, the universe had another gift on top of my Pump and Patterson revelation. I chanced upon a quote by Marion Woodman, a very special woman and Jungian Analyst whom I had heard speak. I met her in person several times, and I had devoured her books. She wrote that

"Children not loved for who they are do not learn to love themselves. Their growth is an exercise in pleasing others, not in expanding through experience."

Her words shot through me like an arrow, a perfect description of me. When I went looking for where that quote was written, I found a small book that Marion wrote with Jill Mellick, Coming Home to Myself. There, another sentence followed the quote: "As adults, they must learn to nurture their own lost child."

Aha! Now, my growth is focused on nurturing my own lost child. I have found someone, a Jungian analyst, to help me learn to do it, and I am alive with curiosity and enthusiasm for the journey.

Since I came to Colorado, I have had two dream figures who have been helpful to me as guides. One, a man, appeared in my dream, standing in my doorway in the dream, dressed in khaki work clothes, leaning against the door frame, just looking in at me. Later, in an active imagination, I asked him what he was doing there, just hanging out in my doorway, looking all beige. He said, "I have come to bring you love and patience." I needed both, for sure. He appears when I need him and reminds me that he is there for me.

Another dream figure I encountered in a dream in which I was in a storied, narrow, and ancient bookstore with a winding many-staircase. I was meandering through, looking at books and about to go up or down another flight, when a man in a wheelchair appeared. He told me, "Hold on, there. You are going with me". Then he put me in his lap in the wheelchair. I asked him where we were going. He said, "To a party," as he rolled toward an elevator that I hadn't noticed. When I later asked him, in an active imagination, what he was doing in my dream, he said he had come to help me "heal the ancient mother wound." I have a mother wound, for sure.

My conversations with each of them are usually written. I ask a question and then wait until I "hear" the answer, and I write that down in my journal. One could say that these are parts of me, or of my inner self, or deeper self, or higher self, or from my unconscious. One or all of those could be true. It doesn't really matter to me when I hear the wisdom that comes.

Years ago, I had a dream in which I was seated on a stone wall with other women. I remember that there were four of us: a very young girl, a young matron, me, and a gray-haired old woman. My therapist asked me if I knew the other ones. I knew a couple and liked them a lot. As we were speaking, I realized they were all parts of me. I was delighted to see that two of them, at least, were women whom I knew in life and admired and to whom I might never have compared myself. I thought they were way cooler in so many ways than I am. That dream came to me around the time of the drumming ceremony. It seemed to be holding up a mirror. I would not have looked if not for the dream.

Chapter Thirteen

As time went on, after Trip's death, I wanted him to *talk* to me. In my heart, I talk to him all the time. Or write to him in my journals. I wanted to find out what he thought about the book I was writing with his name in the title and in whose memory it is being written.

I decided to consult a local medium that I had read about. I have no problem believing there are people who have access to the departed. There are no doubt charlatans, maybe especially on TV, but I know there are those who have an innate ability. Becky, the medium I consulted, is one of those. She says she has been talking with dead people since she was very young. Then she received extensive training, as well, at a school for mediumship.

My experience was positive. Best of all, Trip showed up. Becky told me that Trip had been appearing to her for the past several days before we met, but she didn't know who it was. I had suspected he was doing that. I could picture him dancing around her, making her notice him.

He presented a sort of combo platter of memories of his life and time with me. More were from his youth than I expected.

"I feel lots of energy, lots of intensity from him for you, and lots of emotion. I'm getting that he had a very strong personality (true) and wants you to know that he's here for you, that he's the picture on your phone (also true). He wants to be known, and he's orchestrating this, lots of signs and symbols for you", Becky said. The picture on my phone wasn't there until after Trip's death. I had not shown it to Becky or told her about it. It's a picture of Trip overlooking that place in France that he loved, Calanque d'en Vau, and where I want to deposit the remainder of his ashes.

Early in the session, he wanted me to know that he was gripped by such intensity at the time of his suicide that he did not want me to see into his eyes near the end of his life, to protect me and that there was nothing I could have done to stop him. Hearing his words, I felt both relieved and grief-stricken.

He also wanted me to know that any depression ended with the body. Becky said during this session that his gut felt very tight but that his heart was wide open. That's my Trip. Wide open heart.

He told her I was a beautiful mom and would get down on his level and play with him. He also told her that he wrote thank-you notes and that "Mom taught me to write them". That's true, I did.

The session was much more than I expected. More in the sense that Trip had a lot to say and surprised me with how acutely he had been observing my whole life, especially the time since he died. It was as if he had been seeing or hearing my thoughts and emotions since his death. I guess that's how it is: the dead do observe and hear us. Just for the record, I told Becky nothing other than that I wanted to get in touch with my son, who had taken his own life. What he said made me believe he had been with me in person from his death until this session. The love emanating from him brought forth tears of love and delight. So did his memories of growing up that he sprinkled throughout the session. There was laughter, too.

"I see sandwiches, lots of sandwiches", Becky said, looking puzzled. I began to chuckle. Trip was teasing me. At one time, when the kids were growing up, I made 25 sandwiches every Sunday and put them in the freezer so that each school day, I could pull out five already-made sandwiches for their lunches. I told myself that I was being quite clever to do that. It saved me the rush of doing both breakfast and lunches first thing in the morning. Later, the kids would roast me, saying,

"Oh, Mom, we could never trade those soggy turkey sandwiches with *any*one".

"They weren't *all* turkey", I might say.

Their stories got bigger and more outrageous with each telling, especially if two or more of them were together – even more so if they had an audience who wasn't part of the family.

Another of his memories was an image of the five kids running into the house, ruddy from the outdoors, tracking in dirt galore and running, never walking - lots of energy. And being at the beach the same way, always showing lots of energy and high spirits. That is a composite, but so true in its message. There was always high energy with those five. I relished that, the bordering-on chaos, along with the rest of my life with them.

During the session, when Trip revealed the images meant for me, Becky had to find a way with words to tell me what she was getting. At one point, she got a pain in a rib on her left side that I realized had to do with my having been hurt on an outfitter's bike ride out of the country just a few days before this session. I got too close to the biker in front of me when she was faltering up a hill, and in trying to avoid her, I fell on my left side. My sternum was bruised by the end of the bicycle handlebar when the front wheel turned and hit my chest. I was sore for many days after.

Trip showed Becky his room, which I immediately interpreted as his at-home room from grade school through college until the year Joe and I split and sold the farm. She saw his floor-to-ceiling bookcase and saw Trip pulling out a particular book, a blue hardback one, and holding it up. It caused me to think that he was referring to the one I was writing. Something he showed her led Becky to say, "Trip is a writer, too?" At first, I hesitated, saying, "Not exactly", but as the words came out of my mouth, the light dawned. Of course, Trip is/was a writer, too. The "25 Random Things About Me" that I found on his Facebook page after he died are words that he wrote about himself that show, in his own inimitable way, who he was. Many are in these chapters. He also had a collection of quotes and other comments about his thoughts on life or the state of the world.

"I love the smell of coffee but don't like drinking coffee. I love Reece's peanut butter cups but don't like chocolate alone. The French say that I can never truly be French because I don't love the three C's: Coffee, Cigarettes, and Chocolate."

25 Random Things About Me *#22.* Trip Lucas, Facebook.

He told Becky that he was a catalyst for change in my life and even more so with his death. That astounds me. I have written those same words since his death. Back on the subject in the book, he mentioned *vulnerability* and *raw* and was encouraging me to show that in my writing, to be confident and find my voice. Over and over, he conveyed that I have not always been confident or convinced of my value but that I have had many self-doubts and fears about my own strength as a person or about my abilities. It's true.

Trip saw how I had to be strong for him in his childhood, and he saw that as a beauty in me. He said I was his rock, his *home*. He mentioned several times in different ways that I do have strength and beauty within me. He wants other people to see it, and he wants me to experience it. He said he was persistent as a kid (for sure) and that now he's even more so in wanting me to feel my personal power – be raw, be *strong,* he kept saying. He wanted me to see my own beauty. And he wanted me to know that he's not letting me off the hook for putting myself out there. I assume he meant on the page. He applauded how much I trust my intuition.

Becky said he is bigger than life in the spirit world (an image of the Hulk came to mind), has an energetic presence (which he did in life, too) and wanted me to know that he can exercise his power in big ways for me and feels that he needs to be strong for me.

He said he's aware that I know there's *more,* meaning more than just this material world and life. That pleased him and allowed him to say that it is way big where he is, that his view is expansive - even more than those words can express. I took that to mean he can see the past, present, future, and inside everything and everyone. Or something like that.

He saw flowers all around me and around my house and wanted me to always have lots of flowers, including wildflowers. I do. I have fewer wildflowers than I'd like, but it amazes me that the beautiful Lupine grows wild here, sprouting up everywhere. Columbine are natives, too. I call them the loose women of the plant world. That's because they create new colors with great abandon. How do they do that? They don't appear to be another species of flower, but I haven't investigated this color change propensity. Whatever it is, I welcome them. They can plant themselves in my garden all they want.

He mentioned things like seeing me with a lighted Christmas tree. At mention of that, I told Becky that I have had one outside for over 20 years, that it started when I lived in Virginia. Trip helped me the first time I put the lights on the hemlock tree in my yard. It was at the house where I lived after divorce, the one I called my sanctuary. It was a cozy cape cod and too small for a Christmas tree inside. I got the idea for the outside tree and borrowed a neighbor's old phone company truck with a cherry picker and a man to drive the cherry picker. Trip got up in the bucket to put on the higher lights. When he asked me how I wanted the lights, I said wrapped around each horizontal branch please. Trip didn't quite like that idea – too much work – so he said what he'd do would get across the look.

Becky said, "Yes! That's it, what he showed me, the outside tree!"

He told her that he wants me to continue to celebrate holidays and that it's hard, but that I am coming up with new traditions. Am I? What's interesting to me is that I had no idea during the time I was in Virginia and thought of putting lights on the outside tree that one day I'd be living in a place where lights are up on outside trees all winter. I do try to keep up that tradition.

Becky noticed that Trip had curly hair. He did. That's when I held up the photo on my phone screen of the handsome man with dark curly hair and twinkling blue eyes.

Trip probably saved my life a couple of days before this session with Becky. On the Friday, three days before the session with her, I had flown into Denver after 11 PM. Being the lifelong early bird that I am, I was already way out of my comfort zone by that hour. It still took almost two hours to get my luggage, the shuttle to the parking lot, and then for the brand-new airport shuttle driver to find my car – even though I gave him the parking space number. From there, I drove the twenty-some miles across Denver to where the highway begins to go up toward the high country and about 100 miles left to go. As I started uphill, I began to feel sleepy. So sleepy that I was dozing off. I opened the windows to let the cool night air shock me awake. I shook my head constantly and stuck it almost out the window, but I was still close to nodding off. I started to think about Trip and the upcoming medium session, and that maybe I should just let go, let the car roll off the road, go over the mountain and be done with it, that maybe it was time for me to join Trip. It was then that a sharp voice said, "No! Wake up! Get some coffee!"

I stopped at the next open place and got some peppermints and a cup of bad, lukewarm coffee, but I was starting to wake up. I stopped at another place for some better and very hot coffee, which kept me awake until I arrived home wide awake minutes before 3 AM. Was that Trip's voice I heard? Becky thought so and said, "It sounds as if Trip thinks there's lots more for you to do, and it isn't time for you to go yet."

What I had been led to understand ever since the astonishing revelation at the stop light at the low point of my life almost 40 years ago, I found support in this session with Trip and Becky. What I understood then and still do is that *everything* is connected and here right now. Everything - Past, Present, Future, multi-verses, all of existence. The thing that holds it all together is love.

 Two years after the Becky session, I had this dream:

"As if I've come to a hole-in-the-wall coin or jewelry shop to pick up something I have ordered that will cost $125. I pull out a small round leather coin purse, but the only thing in it is a slightly thin, curved piece of gold that looks as if it is part of one of my earrings. I know I have the money, and so does the man, the shop owner. But I can't find it. A perky little woman goes behind the counter to help me, but she's just another customer. This whole exchange is confusing but friendly, and, in the dream, I *know* it is going to end up well."

The dream reminds me of the original alchemists' quest for a way to turn base metal into gold. The quest is a metaphor for what Jung calls Individuation and is what inspired Jung's deep dive into Alchemy. It makes me feel as if all is going to be well, that the base metal of my life is being turned into gold.

Epilogue

It must mean something, but what? The climbing route, Prototype Wall that led to the spot where the rock bench was placed in Trip's memory, the bench and the bronze plaque that was attached to the bench fell into the Pedernales River. Everything below and around it, the riverbank, climbing route, bench with a plaque in memory of Trip, all disappeared into the river below about five years after Trip's death. The bench was dedicated when we held the memorial service at Milton Reimers Ranch Park in Dripping Springs, Texas.

One of Trip's climbing friends contacted me to let me know and told me that several people asked what they were going to do about the bench and plaque for Trip. I told them that I would purchase another plaque and to let me know when they had decided where to put it. I did that and had the plaque sent to one member of the climbing group who had not climbed with Trip. A year later, the group had still not found the perfect place. When they do, I will provide another plaque.

For now, I have found a home for one on the back of a garden bench that sits in my yard just beyond the patio. It is a special, quiet and shady spot. I can go there any time, have a quiet moment, remember Trip, or talk to him. My now grown dog Bijou often climbs up there with me, and I like to think she remembers Trip, too, since she met him in the first few months of her life.